BE AWARE

Be Aware

<hr>

Ergon-Emotional Intelligence

Josen Olaias

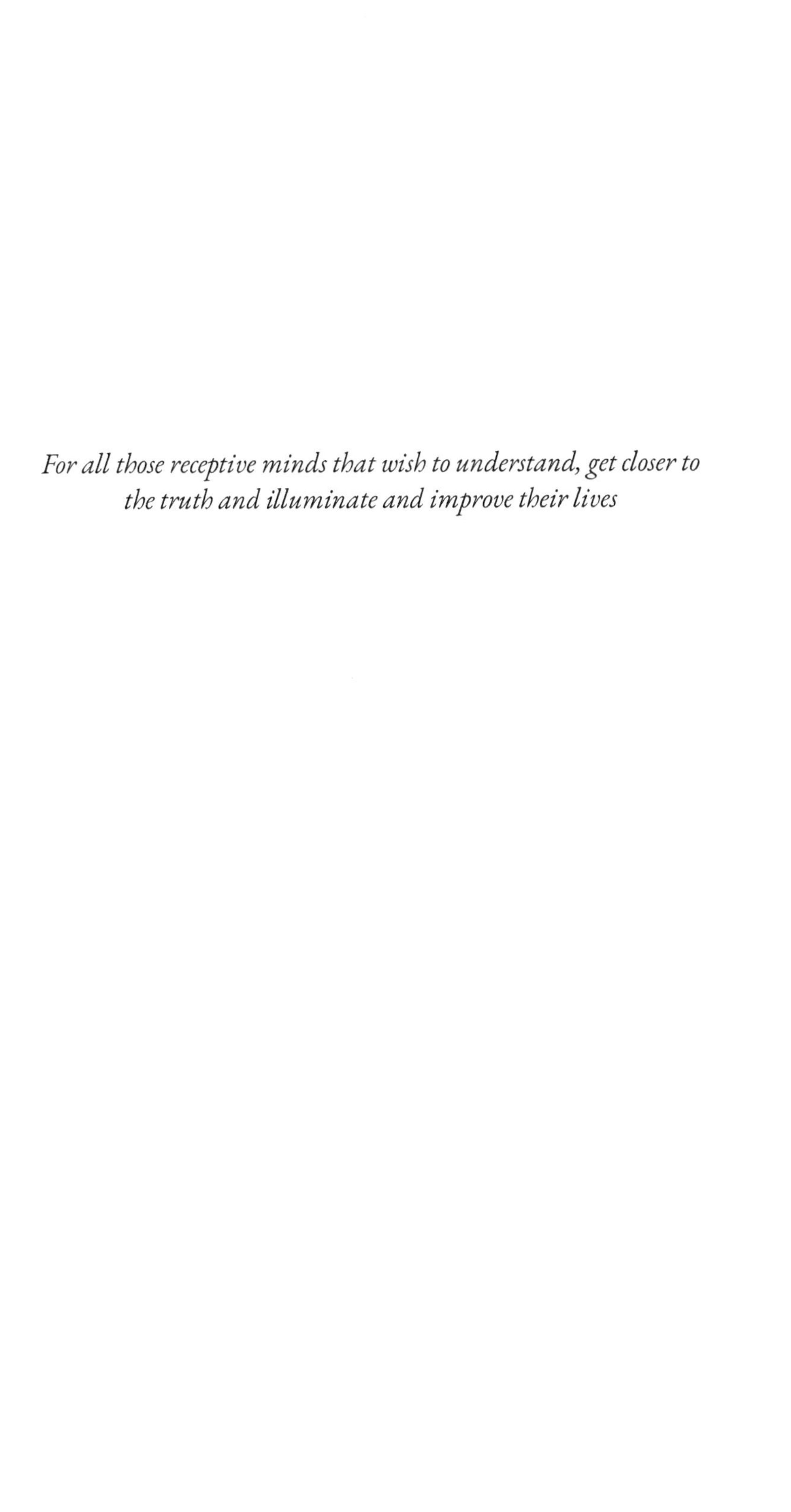

For all those receptive minds that wish to understand, get closer to the truth and illuminate and improve their lives

INTRODUCTION

Curiosity is the inquisitive interest and strong desire to learn, to know and to understand all aspects of life, especially the ones that can be advantageous for us. Even though curiosity can be one of the best allies throughout life, unfortunately, it is the virtue that human beings loses as they grow old. Curiosity can enhance our creativity, promotes our mind activity and it is the cause of many discoveries. I had an experience at an early age that triggered my curiosity, and I'm so thankful for it. I was around the age of three when my grandmother was frying some eggs, and I dropped whole corn in the frying pan and I got popcorn. For me, it was a moment of magic. At that age, I knew what popcorn was, but I did not know that it came from whole corn. Since that moment, I wanted to be in the kitchen all the time, it was like my first laboratory where I could do and create things using my imagination. I was always trying to cook something, pushing the cooks of the family to let me do something. Cooking was my first passion. I also remember when I was around fifteen years old, my neighbour Nora, whose parents were very old, and she used to come and share with me her family issues. I remember that I intent to coach her many times with the little knowledge that I had at that moment. I always remember being young and having the desire to listen to her and try to give her the best advice. Eventually, I went to college, where I finished a degree in science and years later, I ended up opening a restaurant in an old family building, where I use to constantly coach my employees. and at the same time, I started to realize how complex human beings could be. Since then I have dedicated my life to understanding our nature and all those things that affect our well-being. Observing how complicated life could be, and motivated by the need of dealing with employees and the desire to give an excellent service, I started to read books about self-improvement ,which triggered more curiosity about life and how we all can improve ourselves. But at that point in my life, I was living more on the side of fear than on the side of the love, which are the two basic emotions. Therefore, even though I had the best intentions, I was always struggling for not knowing the basic principles of life. In the end, I discovered that to understand our life, it is necessary to understand it in terms of energy, for the simple reason that our spirit is energy and is connected to the rest of the Universe, but they never taught us how our relationship with the Universe work. We are part of the Universe, and we are the Universe. But why such an important topic is not popular among society? To answer this question, it is necessary to dive deep into our history and make our own conclusions. I encourage you to be curious and receptive like I have been.

Another episode of my early life was in the early's 70s when I was around 14years old. There was the newspaper man who delivered the newspapers on his bike, and once a week, he used to come in the afternoon to get his weekly payment and always bring in the basket different magazines. One day, I craved a magazine called Taboo, and my mother let me have it. In that magazine, there were topics like astrology, aliens, numerology and some others, topics that I could not understand at that moment, but I started to learn about the existence of other concepts that I never heard before. I was always eager to learn, ask, understand, and pursue the truth because these are manifestations of curiosity.NowI can conclude and understand clearly that it is dangerous to live our life believing in the definite version. I see the degrees of obstinacy in most people when they hear something against their beliefs or convictions, they prefer to believe and think that is totally right, and the other person is wrong. They prefer to think that you are looking for information in the wrong place. This is a big mistake that most people make unconsciously because of their mental programs. We must be aware that this is the time when we need to be very careful about many things that we have been told and the time to relearn and use our logic and common sense.

When I came to the United States in 2010, I have many bills to pay, and I got a job in a fast-food restaurant earning $35,000 a year. I had the energy and the opportunity of getting a second job to have my own apartment, but I decided to rent a room for many years. Now I look back, and I know that I did what I must do. I had the time to work with myself because I was living a balanced life that permits me to live in calm and spend more time educating myself in many aspects of life. I had the time to start researching more, questioning many things and being able to connect the dots by myself. I learned that we must be careful when it comes to believing without having enough information; living life so naively brings high levels of vulnerability.

I decided to write this book with the main purpose of creating awareness of what we really are and what we have been exposed to, which is nothing more than a powerful indoctrination designed to keep humanity in a collective hypnosis to create the life that few people want. My biggest desire is to see a significant awakening in humanity, where people understand their true nature with Its immeasurable power. Understanding ourselves and taking ownership of our lives is the key to a better life. This book is a guide towards a personal transformation where anyone can understand their life and learn how to create a better reality.

This book is written in a simple way to understand different concepts that are going to be the foundation for a good life and help you to have your own criteria, not the criteria that others want you to have. It is possible to put all the pieces together and improve our understanding of ourselves and our life. I want to help to direct lives toward a better direction and live it with more logic and common sense, and the most important, learn to validate ourselves without the interferences of limiting beliefs. This is the time to acknowledge a new way of thinking, is the moment to expand our mind, otherwise we will not be able to achieve the positive changes that we all want. I think that a new cliché should be "If you want to change your life, you should change the way you think". It is time to understand what we really are, understand our essence and understand the force that moves everything called energy. Throughout the book, I repeat quite a few concepts over and over with the idea to stick it in your mind.

CHAPTER 1

All institutional structures have influenced people since the beginning of time. Bringing misinformation to deliberate control of the planet. They always have been deviating our attention from any beneficial information; they even ridicule the topics they intend to keep secret. We have been living our lives accepting lies, secrets, wars, segregation, diseases, anguish, and stress as something normal without wandering why. People unconsciously support the system constantly without realizing that is a system based on fears, lies, distraction and even human degradation Most people defend the system, understanding that being obedient is to be responsible, which is totally absurd, because we are not quite sure who we have been obeying to. They are always directing us to the opposite side of what can be beneficial for us.

My writing is straight to the point. I consider that we do not need to much narrative to explain things. My intention is not to attack it is to create awareness and pursue the truth. I recommend opening your mind, be reasonable and use your logic and common sense. Throughout the book, I carry two different topics at the same time. One topic is about your nature, and the other one is to understand all the external things to which we have been exposed. You must understand how important it is to work with our true being, from where our experiences are created and also recognize that it is not just about believing. It is about understanding with sensibleness. It is the responsibility of each one of us to explore beyond the formal statement. Therefore,I must tap sensitive topics with the intention of connecting the dots. This book is to understand yourself and your life. It is to validate humanity and take them out of the powerless scheme, where we need to prioritize between knowledge and beliefs. I can perceive a red flag when comes to believing without understanding. **You need to be aware** that if you want to have assertive conclusions and make the right decisions, a broad spectrum of information is fundamental. I want this book to be as precise as possible, straight to the point, easy to read, and efficient in opening people's minds. Here, I express all the useful information I have gathered since childhood and all the concepts that have helped me to create a better life. My main intention is to lift human beings and help them understand the inner power that resides in each one of us. After all these years of researching, I dare to say that many essential concepts have been taught the other way around with an outrageous purpose. You just need to look at the tendencies of deterioration around our planet. We are used to accepting many odd things as normal because of not having enough information, but we don't have to accept it as normal to have complicated lives where struggling and despair are very common. I now know that life can be more harmonious for everyone if every human being decides to embrace the intention of becoming better and pursue the knowledge that bring empowerment. We need to be humble to accept new ideas and concepts and have the courage to face traditional actions established by the institutions around us. We are having auspicious moments to raise awareness and uplift our spirit. It is the moment to be brave, fight for our true ideals, and validate ourselves. But we need to accept that we wall are part of the collective hypnosis, understanding that hypnosis is this state of mind where your peripheral awareness is reduced, and your capacity to respond to suggestion is enhanced. Washing television is probably the most effective tool to influence people, and lately, it is extremely aggressive programming people's minds.

Television is a harmful weapon; besides distracting us, it is always programing our subconscious mind. Every time we watch television,, we are under the influence of other people's opinions, and we are in a mental state where we are not free to see the world for ourselves. Every time we watch television, we are in some level of hypnosis, which is the right mental state to be programmed. Scientists know that changes occur on a neurological level when we are exposed to tv for prolonged periods of time. Watching tv can change how much we use certain brain areas and how these brain regions develop. I can observe the difference between the ones that don't watch tv and the ones that watch tv. The ones that do not watch tv are more receptive to assimilate new ideas and concepts, and they are even healthier and happier people and more productive. On the other hand, the ones who watch a lot of TV tend to be more antisocial, stubborn, less healthy, and have an altered brain structure. Be aware that we are constantly receiving messages that influence our behavior, and this one always needs adjustments.

When we observe some behaviors in past generations. and how things have been changing throughout time, help us to recognize and understand the importance of changing. For example, in the middle age, probably one of the darkest moments in human history, we saw the devastation caused by the Black Plague and the death and destruction caused by the Crusades. During this period, it was believed that wearing an amulet containing a weasel (ferret like animal) testicle would prevent pregnancy.

In the Century 17th, tea was generally considered a lady's drink and often consumed by the mistress of the house and her friends. Also, people used to think sperm contained tiny human beings. Even in the last century, scientists believed that neurons did not have the capacity to regenerate. Now, science recognizes the neurogenesis. These are just a few examples of how humanity, at some point, always understands that they are doing and thinking in the right way. If we observe, humans have always lived with a certain level of ignorance, but curiosity always exists to help us find better ways to do things and live in better conditions. How do we judge our past generations? How future generations could judge ourselves? We have evolved from those times, but we continue to live in darkness. It is time to acknowledge change and be more receptive to the possibility to live in a brighter world full of opportunities. Being curious is probably one of the biggest assets in our society because curiosity means expansion and progress. Everything we can imagine can be created with the right mindset. But we have an obstacle, which is a malfunction of our minds. This malfunction has been provoked by the leadership of our planet with the purpose of having power over humanity. When more people start to fix their mental weaknesses, opening their minds to new information and practicing it, everything on the planet will start to get better. I guarantee that at the end of the book, you will understand with logic and common sense why things can get better in your life and in the planet. However there are many questions to be answered and analyzed.

For example, Why one of the first things we hear is that we are sinful and imperfect, instead of telling us that our spirits are energy and that energy is made of photons, which are particles of light and acknowledge that we have a divine nature with an infinite power? They also should have told us that our energy is connected to the rest of the Universe and suggested you learn and understand how to apply the Basic Principles of the Universe to our life. But they did the opposite, they are constantly attacking our true being, breaking down our internal power, implanting guilt and inferiority complexes among humanity to create distortion in our connection with the creative source. This is a serious situation, and **we need to be aware.**

We are constantly creating the reality that others want. But this is the time of the great awakening. Opening your mind is a requisite to enhance your infinite power. It is time to understand what we really are. The process of understanding and assimilating our divine nature requires effort and courage, we need to reset our subconscious mind, change mental habits, and have an active determination of what you really want. But we need to keep in mind that change is an ongoing process.

It is good to understand the importance of change as a constant process in our lives. There are so many aspects of our history that can help us to recognize things that we never imagined. Facts that will help to open your mind and become more receptive, considering that receptive means being willing to receive. We all want to receive material things, but the most important thing we need to receive is knowledge and apply it to our life, giving way to a balanced one, where we can have control of your existence.

When I was around thirteen years old, after watching my family discussing and arguing for something that I don't remember right now, I decided to keep my mind open as much as I can. I decided not to be like them. At that early age I could understand that the problem in that family discussion was that one of my grandparents was not able to understand my parent's points of view. Now, after so many years is clear for me to see how most people become less receptive as they grow older, and this is an unconscious behavior that affect all kind of relationships. Why do people become so stubborn as the grow old? The main reason could be the programs that we unconsciously receive in the daily basis. Some of that information is design to create fanatics and stubborn people. Being aware of how your mind is fed every day by information designed to create the reality that just a few people want, it is crucial to accept that you have the responsibility of becoming more conscious about everything that surround you. The process of becoming unconsciously close-minded starts when people accept information with out analyzing it with logic and common sense, many times, there is no congruence between what we have been told and what is really happening. We need to question, inquire, and analyze everything. Most people are extremely distracted that never have the time to analyze information with a rational mind, they just follow the official version, which, most of the time, is all twisted to support a shady agenda. We all should make a commitment to never lose our curiosity, always remembering when, at some point we all have had experiences with extremely stubborn people in denial to accept concepts even though the facts are logical. At any age, we can be stubborn, but as we grow old, there is a high possibilities to close our minds and fall into the trap of obstinacy. Being stubborn is probably one of the biggest problems in society. "Obstinacy kills curiosity, and when we kill our curiosity, we are killing our inner child, and that is the moment when you start a mental decline. Avoid stubbornness at all costs. We need to be aware of this and constantly observe and understand that someday, we are going to grow older and can have the same problem. Some people who are reading this right now might think that everybody else have the problem except me, but this is a general situation that belongs to everyone of us; all of us have been mentally affected by the same information. At some point, when I heared talking about people issues, wrong behaviors and ways of being, I immediately say to myself, there are many possibilities that I have the same issues because I am part of the people, and I am receiving the same information. When we start observing ourselves and acknowledging our unconscious behaviors, it is the moment when we really start to work with ourselves and improving our situation. How many times are we paying attention to our behavior? Everybody is receiving the same information to be like they want us to be, stubborn, powerless, fearful, submissive, obedient, and distracted as much as possible. Why everyone is afraid of being wrong? The reason is that we all carry with many childhood programs where we were punished for being wrong, like when we get a bad grade in a test. Everybody love to look like they know instead of being more receptive. Every time we say I know; we are probably missing an opportunity to get new information. Unfortunately, most people follow what is common in society.

The ambition or need to accomplish society's standards like

study, get a job, get married, have children, have a house etc. and of course teach your children the same limiting beliefs you learn, is the trap where most people fall. All these behaviors are unconscious because we tend to trust whatever has been established by the institutions of the planet. Being focus on achieving goals and not practicing self-observation is another trap. How many times do we stop and think about ourselves and our lives and wonder why, if we have so many resources and technology on this planet, things are going worse or why sometimes it gets so complicated? Have you asked yourself why, after age of 50, so many people start having health issues, look how everybody is going in the same direction as they grow old. We don't need so much evidence to know what's really going on on the planet, we just need to take some time and analyze it. I don't think it is fair to struggle all your life to end up living in pain and scarcity why there is so much lack in some African countries when Africa is full of natural resources? How much time we have spent researching about our beliefs and the institutions that we follow? Everybody wants to be a good human being, but not everybody practices the things they need to practice to become their best self. If our life is not what we want, it is because we are not believing and practicing the right things. Human beings need to feel accepted by society, and it is easier to think like everybody else, than goes against what has been established, and this is another trap. Human beings need to sense that they belong to the herd other than being rejected, which does not feel good. The consequence of this unconscious behavior is that we are neglecting our inner- self and passing our power to others. Pain, scarcity, anguish, and distractions are part of a design.

CHAPTER 2

Distractions are our worse enemy. How many times a day we need to remember that? All the time. We need to remember it constantly, otherwise, you will never be out of the **harmful distraction**. How do you spend your time? How many hours are you connected to devices, watching tv shows, playing video games etc? The more distracted you are, the more influenced you are to behave like a few people want, deviating you from what truly matters and therefore provoking mental chaos that resides in most people mind. If we are always distracted, we will never have time to analyze and use our common sense, neither time to connect with ourselves, or our essence where your infinite power resides. Everything is designed to keep us disconnected from the divine source. We have been receiving the same official information, which is not quite clear, information that is very well planned and designed to close people's minds and many other things. We have always been diverted from any information beneficial to us, and even sent to the opposite side of what is favorable for us. Think about how many concepts in our society are based on fear and separation, observe the news constantly shooting people with negativity. When you analyze that love and fear are the two basic emotions, fear provoking a low energy vibration and love uplifting your vibration, it is obvious that something odd is happening around us. If you are in fear, you are more vulnerable to living in lack, with health issues, feeling powerless and demoralized, therefore, more manipulable and obedient you are going to be Why is the system based on fear and not on love and unity?

When I got divorced at my 44years old I decide to stop watching TV, and I started reading more and having more time in silence with myself. I was always reading a book about self-improvement. I had time to investigate all kinds of topics: history, health, emotional intelligence, quantum physics, and neuroscience. I started to learn, expand and observe myself, which has been a long process, and I feel that there is a long way to go when we want to master consciousness, self- awareness and mindfulness. As a result of living life with more curiosity and spending my time constructively, my actual life is harmonious and balanced, which I consider foundations of wellbeing. I can compare my life now with my life 21 years ago after my divorce and the journey has been long, but the results are worth it. I have been experiencing an improvement in my self- esteem, confidence, health and finances.

I moved to the United States, at the age of 51 years, understanding that I must work with fears and limiting beliefs, but with a strong conviction about improving my life. At that moment as an employee with plenty of time and a laptop in my hands I kept feeding myself with all kinds of information that could help me improve myself. On the other hand, I was struggling with intestine problems, since I was diagnosed Chron's disease at age 27, and in the past, I had a few crises where doctors even wanted to cut my intestines, but inside of me I always knew that it was not necessary. Being in a process of change and emotionally unbalanced it is obvious that I could not be in optimal health, but I was committed to improve my life as much as I could. I remember that somewhere I read that life changes are like turning the transatlantic ship's rudder very fast, but the ship is going to move very slow. I know it was my journey and my story, I decided to be patient while starting to fall in love with knowledge. I kept reading books and watching all kinds of videos about many topics that show up in front of me. I started to improve my knowledge about new ideas, as well as important information to work with my life. As of today, I no longer have Chron's disease or any type of health issues, and I achieved this by getting rid of limiting beliefs, validating myself and improving my emotional states. As I worked with my inner self and developed a better connection with my higher self I started to enjoy the wonders of the divine source. One of the most authentic intentions is the desire to understand, know the truth and work with your life and your inner being.

We all make mistakes, but one of the most common mistakes is ,live our lives believing in everything we have been told without questioning or investigating. Not many people ask questions, they prefer to give their opinions, that, most of the time are based on little and twisted information. We need to understand that many things that we hear throughout life and repeat them as correct, are not necessarily correct. Is time to run our life with more reasoning and common sense. We need to remember that many things that we do every day like taking decisions, purchases, and accepting beliefs are based in emotions. Emotions play an important role in how our life is manifested, it is good to mention that our emotions are also stored in your subconscious mind and this one has been exposed to many external programs that go against our wellbeing. Many time people experience the fear of letting go of ideas or convictions and develop mental rigidity which disturbs our progress.

We are living in a society full of stubborn and fearful human beings that cannot move up, even though everyone have a desire to have a better life. I remember when I found the principle of the law of attraction, it was like an aha moment. I was excited about the concept because it resonates with me significantly, and I wanted to share it with everybody, but I received lots of rejection. It was when I started asking myself why people are so stubborn, and I am still observing this common behavior, trying to figure out what kind of information people receive that makes them so stubborn. Probably one of the main causes is our limiting beliefs, which are always interfering with our perception, avoiding recognizing a world full of possibilities. How many times do we hear something that goes against our convictions or beliefs and immediately shoot back to defend our position without giving ourselves any opportunity to wonder. Probably a good solution for this bad habit is to program ourselves to always ask, instead of shoot back within a second. For example, we can ask: Why do you say that? Do you have good arguments to support your statement? Do you really believe in that? Why? What kind of resources do you use to inform yourself How long you been researching about it? Open-minded people always ask, closed minded ones shoot back. Paying more attention to your reactions is the way out of the harmful pattern of being stubborn. Paying more attention to our mental processes should be a daily practice being these mental processes the ones that determine our emotional states. If we really want to become an authentic good person, we need to work with ourselves as much as we do in our regular job, it must be our priority and our new healthy habit. We need to live with more curiosity and flexibility and pay more attention to our reactions. Working with ourselves means being more mindful, we need to dedicate more time to observe how we really are, examine our actions, reactions, thoughts, feelings, perceptions, intentions, and emotions; self-exploration is the name of the game. Working with ourselves and our mental processes is working with our inner being therefore we can make adjustments in our daily life. How do we manage our spare time? How productive do we think we are? Think about that. I can understand the importance of taking a break from our daily tasks and relax but we need to organize and prioritize activities during our spare time to be aware of what kind of life we are constantly creating. Nobody is so busy for not taking care of themselves, it is a matter of priorities. Our actual life is a result of all our habits, physical, mental, and emotional and these in turn are the result of your thoughts and beliefs, which some of them are destructive and limiting. But why it is like this?

Facts to be analyzed

The first time I heard that history helps us to understand our present I thought that I understood, like we usually do, but never thought how powerful and meaningful it was until I heard in a conference that the Old Testament is a twisted edition of the Sumerians Text. Next day, I started my investigation into the forbidden story of the Sumerians, our first civilization. Legitimate information has been on the planet since the beginning, but it was suppressed. Sumer was a civilization that emerged organized, a civilization with fewer rules, living in unity and harmony, with social equality, where everybody deserves to know and have anything. The story was so incredible that I probably spent more than 300 hours to acquire all possible details. I remember during that process, I was obsessed with trying to understand better all that strange story. I was basically all day and night looking for more information about it. I used to ask myself why I was so obsessed with it. Eventually, I understood that it was necessary to understand that story so that I could understand many things about our present moment. It was the moment when I started to understand what's really going on on this planet. Sumerian history is like a science fiction story, but our reality surpasses fiction. There is enough archeology and forbidden archeology to demonstrate many facts that put in evidence what probably happened at the beginning of time. The Sumerian's history is basically a story of aliens. The biggest proof is all the pyramids around the world, where we have so many theories about their construction but nothing specific. We have always heard that with today's technology, its construction would be impossible. But we are so distracted that we have never given importance to who built them, believing in theories created by men with the purpose of deviating us from reality. It is out of logic to understand that we are the only ones in the Universe what is logic is to understand that as below, so above. Another evidence of advanced creatures on the planet is the Ooparts (out of place artifacts), which are artifacts of advanced technology dating back thousands of years. These artifacts let us know that thousands of years ago, technologically advanced creatures were in our planet. If we cannot understand certain information, we will never be able to connect the dots with logic and common sense.

The Sumerian tablets, the first writings of mankind, let us know about a civilization that left quite a few legacies like the first writing (cuneiform), mathematics, navigation, and agriculture. They are also considered the first brewers and many other things. During that time, spirituality and science were a blend, which is logical considering that our spirit is energy, so we must understand how our energy behaves in relation to the Oneness of the Universe. The Sumerian story also lets us know that the alien's race named was Anunnaki which, were channeling the rivers Tigris and Euphrates, when at one point, they needed working hands and decided to make a slave, genetically modifying the Neanderthal man and the homo erectus with their reptilian race. The story has two main characters, Enki and Enlil, which were half-brothers. Enlil parents were both draconian reptilian and Enki's mother was a benevolent race. Enlil was like a military chancellor, and Enki was the geneticist who spent quite a few thousand years doing all kind of mischief until he finally creates the homo sapiens and fall in love with humans. He even wants to bring humans through the process of illumination (opus magnum), but Enlil opposed it, and the conflict between the brothers started. Enlil, with all his power and technology provoked the great flood, and Enki was the one who contacted Ziusudra to rescue the people. Eventually, the Akkadians, our second civilization already controlled by the Enlil, began to infiltrate Sumer, creating conflicts until they absorbed the Sumerians, and our first civilization disappeared, leaving behind a considerably amount of archaeology items that clearly tells us that many of the official stories are incorrect. Since that moment, our planet has been governed under a domination system, where they always use the same strategy of mixing facts with lies and demonizing the good ones. The sensitive fact in this story is that Enlil is the God of the Old Testament, Enki is the Lucifer, and Ziusudra is Noah. The story of the Sumerians is basically the same story of the Old Testament with different names and a twist to favor the bad and demonize the good. Analyze how the God of the Old Testament likes human sacrifices and other weird things. But the most terrifying fact is that a faction of this negative entity (Enlil-Jehovah) is what has been ruling the planet since then. A conspiracy theory? I don't think so? What is real is a conspiracy against humanity, but I don't think it is a theory. I know this is a story hard to believe for many people, but at this point, I have observed that it resonates for some people and not for others, but it is the responsibility of each one to investigate. When we research this topic, we also find many other pieces of information that help us to connect the dots and have our own criteria, not the criteria that others want us to have by giving us twisted information. We need to understand and accept that we have been living in a big lie all our lives, we need to let go many limiting beliefs otherwise, the process of improving our lives will be slow or none. On the other hand, in the bible, Enki was that angel that was next to God but went against his will. Here, we can discern it is the same strategy; they are still using these days. The bad is the good one, and the good one is the bad one. Observe how in these days the politicians who love to kill people in unnecessary wars are supposed to be the good ones, and they use all their power to demonize the politicians who don't like to sponsor wars. Always use the same strategies, creating chaos, demonizing, and mixing facts with lies.

I dare to say that religions are dark cults where humans are sinners and imperfects, sons of God but are not gods instead we must be servants of God. I want to say again: why one of the first things they tell you is that we are imperfect and sinful instead of telling us that our spirit is energy, energy that is connected to the rest of the Universe, made of photons, which are particles of light? We are light beings with a divine nature and infinite potential. If we are a light beings and part of the Universe, we are perfect. Probably, the general meaning of perfection is kind of twisted as well. Perfection is balance. When you consider the duality of the Universe, positive and negative are always coexisting; one cannot exist without the other. Observe the symbol of Yin and Yang, where a circle is made up of black and white swirls, each containing a spot of the other. If everything is good, there is no balance. What is not perfect is the way we were taught to think.

When we analyze religions and realize that they don't emphasize how to work with our inner world and do the opposite, inducing people to be distracted with the otter world they evidently are directing people to the opposite side of what is convenient for us. This is not about attacking religions; this is about pursuing the truth with logic and common sense and validating what we really are. If we have an original book and make another book based on that original, in which I twisted facts and events and changed the names of the characters, which book holds the truth? The answer is up to you.

Let's analyze Christianity and Jesus with a message of love and empowerment and with the opposite behavior of Enlil- Jehovah, that was a demanding God. In the beginning, Christians were persecuted probably for the positive message of Jesus, and considering that the planet was already under this system of domination it is evident that Jesus's message of empowerment was counterintuitive, therefore Emperor Constantine looking for power and with the same behavior. Of pharaoh Akhenaton who to acquire power started monotheism in Egypt, decided to establish Christianism as a strategy to reunify the Roman empire where most of the roman population was already Christian. Taking advantage of this, they took over the history and teachings of Jesus and used them to their benefit. The Christianism was growing by imposition throughout hundreds of years of conditioning people, with military expeditions called the Crusades and the Holy Inquisition torturing, killing people and destroying and hiding any knowledge that was against their doctrine. All this terror has been transmitted from generation to generation, keeping people in a turbulent emotional state. Does it really make sense to follow movements created by criminal politicians? Observe how these politicians also create a story about Jesus that doesn't make much sense. The premise that he died on the cross for our sins is totally absurd. Our journey through life is a personal experience. Besides, it is a message about sacrificing for others and subliminally tells that suffering is a good thing. Sacrificing for others does not make any sense. Each one journey and evolution is an individual process. The Christianity and all religions bring a subliminal message of humiliation and impotence. After all these years of investigation I cannot tell exactly if Jesus existed or not, but I'm inclined to believe in his existence, but what I'm pretty sure is that if he existed the history we have been told is not quite precise. But we always can accept his message of love and empowerment, not the patterns of sacrifice and suffering, which carry a low frequency vibration. An odd fact about Jesus is the famous painting by Michelangelo, the paint of Jesus that we used to see in our grandmother's houses. The model that Michaelangelo used for the image of Jesus was his lover Tommaso De Cavalieri. When you talk about this sensitive topic people don't want to listen, they just want to be right and is understandable after thousands of years of indoctrination based in fear and restrictions against our inner self. My intention is to get people out from the mental comfort zone and persuade them to reevaluate their beliefs and analyze if is logic to follow institutions that were stablished shedding blood. It does not make too much sense to work with my spirituality, putting my attention outside when everything starts from within. Beside why, you must pass your power to a superior being and fall into the belief that we are powerless, thinking that our life is as God wishes. The real God, Divine Source, Universe, has nothing to do with that cruel and terrifying God of the Old

Testament. The purpose of creating God was to generate fear among humans and suppress our inner power. How many times you have heard "fear to God"? Does it really make sense? If God is love, why we must be afraid of him? On the other hand, Hebrews 12 28-29 says, "Therefore let us be grateful for receiving a kingdom that cannot be shaken, and thus lets us offer to God acceptable worship, with reverence and awe, for our God is a consuming fire." Why consuming fire? Why so much reverence? Observe the message of submission and fear, which is already imprinted in people's subconscious minds.

I already have seen many people distracted with God all their lives, they never learn to quite their minds, always worrying and living in fear, In the end I can see the last ten or twenty years of their lives are a total disaster, living in pain and despair. I want to say it repeatedly: they been always deviating us from the correct path. Observe how many people believe in God and observe how many people have miserable lives because of not believing in their inner power and support concepts created by criminals. The power is within each of us. The concept of God is based in the Universe; both are infinite omnipresent, and we are made in the image and likeness of God because we are intelligent energies that are connected to the Universe. Analyze the bible and observe how cruel was that God always demanding and asking for things in return. Light beings will never ask for anything in return, they just guide us in a very subtle way. Personally, I can use the term God as something cultural, but I prefer not to sponsor something that causes so much separation and conflict and specially when I understand what it implies in terms of energy, I don't want to be energetically related or connected to so much segregation, suffering, despair and even wars. Believing in God or being Christian does not mean that we are good human beings. I prefer the Universe that supports unity and gives me basic principles that bring me a clear understanding about life, spirituality and my purpose.

Religion versus spirituality

Religion is not just one; there are hundreds, spirituality is just one. Religion is for the sleeping ones; spirituality is for those who want to awaken. Religion is for those who need to be told what to do and want to be guided, spirituality is for those who pay attention to their inner voice. Religion has a set of dogmatic rules, and spirituality invites us to reason and question everything. Religion threatens and scares, spirituality brings inner peace. Religion talks sin and guilt; spirituality tells learn from our mistakes. Religion represses everything and makes you fake; spirituality transcends everything and makes you true. Religion invents; spirituality discovers. Being religious does not make you spiritual, not many religious people reach a high level of spirituality, and this is tangible. You just need to observe most people's conditions, besides you can see the attitude of most religious people when it is hard to them to accept new ideas and concepts.

Now that I see so much useful information, beneficial for improving people's lives and understanding that this information was in our planet since the beginning of times, I cannot believe in any institution of this planet. For example, analyze religions they give hope to people, but at the same time, they instill, guilt, sacrifice, and submission. Religions are practical to a certain point but do not really help people that much. If they were so efficient in fixing people's life, people would leave the churches, just like the medical industry where they relief people pain but don't really heal that many people, besides the unnecessary surgeries and the intoxication of patients with medicines that have side effects. Why do medicines have side effects when nature has many ingredients to heal without harming people's bodies, and there is so much technology available? The same happened with governments with their social departments that really help people, but they are always creating segregation, unnecessary wars and spending a lot of time and money on unimportant things, and of course, educational institutions teaching people to be obedient working bees. All institutions on the planet are on the same page and need to follow the nefarious agenda against humanity. Observe all the energy and money they during the COVID-19, but decade by decade there is around 8 -10 million children disappear in the world, and they don't put much effort into solving that situation. When I found this information about the missing children, I could not believe the amount and decided to investigate the number of missing children around the world. And when I start adding the amounts from country to country, they is probably more than10million. We need to live with courage and stop accepting all the falsities of the system where fear is their favorite tool to keep humanity under control. It is for sure a system of domination and degradation of humankind, where your subconscious mind is programmed to create fearful and weak people not the opposite. The solution to this problem resides within each one of us, deciding what to accept and prioritizing working and developing our true selves.

Another point to analyze is how, at the beginning, church and government were joined, and these politicians were criminals ,torturing and killing people to establish Christianism and other religions. Where the fear of that moment has been transmitted from generation to generation. Understanding that since the second civilization we have been under a system of domination, it is obvious to understand that everything started with corrupt politicians, as today, we must have corrupt politicians. If everything had started with honest politicians, today, we would have honest politicians. They would never have allowed evil to prevail. Do you really believe that it is logical to follow and believe in corrupt politicians who have been killing people and creating chaos since the beginning? We always have been supporting and defending criminals, and the worst part, is supporting the darkness. But probably the most important fact is that our planet is ruled by negative entities that feed themselves from our low frequency emotions. That is why it is important for the rulers of the planet to keep humanity in constant chaos. What we all want is love, unity, freedom, and happiness, not so much segregation and confusion. And I ask to myself, at the end, who is right Christians, Muslims, Jews, or the Hindus with their thousand's gods?

If, at the beginning, church and government were united means that the Bible was design by politicians, not by spiritual people. I can understand clearly that the Bible is a book of social engineering, and probably what people call the prophecies of the Bible are basically an agenda that must be executed. I know this might be hard to swallow for many people, but there are so many facts that point in that direction. In the end each religion has its own book adjusted to its needs. Ahh, and all those books with a terrifying god.

Everything is obvious but hard to assimilate for many people; facts like these activate cognitive dissonance and confirmation bias. In other words, it causes discomfort and rejection. I recommend analyzing, investigating, and pursuing the truth. We all carry many limiting and destructive beliefs established by the institutions of the planet, and those beliefs are constantly holding people back. I recommend to acknowledging the lies and the limiting beliefs and having the courage to start accepting new concepts that can help to improve your life. Our transformation process starts changing our mind-set and becoming another person. If we are not honestly satisfied with our lives and our surroundings, it means that we are not believing and practicing the right things, and this just happens because of the misinformation we are constantly receiving and accepting. Living in lack, always worrying and being unhealthy is a design. I know it is unbelievable, but we have been living under mental control ever since. The process of acceptance is difficult, especially for older people, but it is necessary and very profitable to have the courage and humility to start accepting the falsehood we have been living in Recognize the importance of a change of mentality should be our priority. Otherwise, we will continue making the same mistakes and having the same thoughts and behaviors that create the situations we are experiencing right now. Another example of how we have been deprived of knowledge is when you discover that at the beginning of times, astrology, which is a tool from the Universe to provide guidance during our life journey and was used to help people in their decisions, was considered a cosmic or a divine science, and was eventually converted it in astronomy, a materialistic science and rule by an institution. The same happened with alchemy, which was turn into chemistry, another materialistic science. Those are examples of how we always have been directed to the opposite side of what is beneficial for us. Everything on the planet is altered. We all have enough evidence that our planet is not ruled by the best people. It is just that we are so distracted that we do not pay attention to the evidence that surrounds us. Why do you think the entertainment industry is so powerful? We are conducted to be constantly distracted; the system wants to decide everything for us. People need to learn to say no. Most humans spend most of their lives trying to achieve what is established by society and never realize how everyone is immersed in distractions, forgetting to take care of their inner being, their essence, and their nature.

Do you think that the people who, from the beginning, have been killing people in unnecessary wars of their own making are telling us the truth and really care about us? Observe how, from the beginning there have always been wars, wars created with intention by the same governments. We can analyze the never-ending conflict between Israel and Palestine originated from religious motivations. It is logical to think that most of the people of these countries prefer to live in peace and forget whether Jerusalem belongs to Palestine or not. This conflict started in 1948 with the intention to perpetuate the conflict and keep that region in constant anguish.It comes to my mind why there is so much chaos in that area where our civilization started? Do they need to keep destroying some kind of evidence that clarifies what really happened at the beginning of humanity? And even worse, terrorism is financed by the same governments, always creating chaos to keep people divided and in fear, which is the best strategy for people control. We just need to look around us and use our logic and common sense. So much money is spent in wars and so many people living in inhumane situations. We need to be more reflective about the events around us, always understanding that being obedient and being responsible with ourselves are different things, especially when we don't really know who we are obeying. As I mentioned before, many information we receive is backwards.

We have been wired to believe without understanding. Since childhood you start learning and assimilating many things and we follow them without asking, understanding that adults are right, but with no idea of the manipulation to which they have all been subjected. There is a story about a young boy that asked to her mother why she fry the fish without head, and she replies that's the way I learned, ask your grandmother. So, the boy went and asked his grandmother, and she reply I don't know ask your grand grandmother, the boy went and ask her, and the answer was, "because back in the days we were so poor, so the frying pan was too small and the whole fish did not fit in". Always following others without questioning is not the best idea, of course being too curious is not well seen in society. I always remember when I was growing up everybody use to tell me all the time "the curiosity killed the cat". Now I would say "I prefer to die but knowing".

An example of how they twist everything is the 2012 event where the popular information was about the Mayans' prophecies and the end of the world, but they never mention that the real event was the end of a cycle where our solar system was coming out to the light, after been approximately 12,800years in the darkness (galactic night).Logical to understand that during those years of darkness was when institutions like governments, religions and secret societies get started. What happened on December 21, 2012, was the first day of the galactic day, when the whole solar system started to receive the light from the sun of the galaxy and this event is going to last another 12,800years. This event means that humanity is in a process of a significant awaking. It is very curious that I found out this information in 2013, and there was plenty of information out there about this topic, but eventually, this information disappeared for quite a few years, then in 2022, I found it again. Maybe they are busy censoring other kind of information and forgot about this one. As you can see, information is always manipulated to create confusion in humanity. This event is telling us that these are auspicious moments for a global awakening.

Another example to analyze is how, in the 1990s there were many corporations that have the control of the communication industry around the planet after the Telecommunication Act were signed, with the fake goal to lead to competition and private investment and promoting universal service and open access to information networks.But something unexpected happened the number of media corporations started to go down. Currently, there are only six corporations that control 90% of the information around the planet and basically all of them are on the same page. Something It should be alarming also frightening to know that the owners of these corporations are very well connected with the same goal toward humanity. This is the time where we must understand that any official information could be twisted with the purpose of human control. Even the fact checkers sites are controlled by the powerful ones, and their fight against "misinformation" is getting very aggressive and. I ask myself, If the information out of the official version is not true, why they are so worried? Remember, they are always directing people in the opposite direction of what may be good for humanity. We just need to observe around us and ask to ourselves, why so much chaos and suffering all the time?

But information is more accessible to everyone, we just need to get out of the useless distractions and spend some time searching for the information that permit us to have our own criteria. Remember, a person who is receptive always asks and investigates. The stubborn ones are distracted with meaningless activities and shoot you back to defend their points of views with copy-paste arguments. In other words, they are just repeating what they have heard without any investigation. Investigation is an ongoing process, we need to be more responsible with ourselves, reasoning, wondering, and questioning any idea that move the mass of people so we can know what kind of things we are supporting. I need to repeat it, we need to stop living life so naively. When you decide to investigate, you must consider whether you are investigating to be right or to know the truth and understand.

Conspiracy theories are very controversial, but what I have been observing is that any information that goes against the official version is a conspiration theory, which is a term that the CIA popularized after the JFK murder to ridicule anyone who gets out of the official version or tries to find out the truth. In 2022, a friend sends me an article from The New York Times titled "Why people believe in conspiracy theories". According to the article, from an investigation team in Atlanta (they are not too specific about the origin of the article, which is a red flag) classifies conspiracists as people with mental disorders, as usual, always diminishing those that want to know the truth. But the reality is that people are awakening and have more information available to have their own criteria. This is about being more responsible with the information we receive and stop thinking that everything we hear comes from the horse's mouth.

If you look for the term New World Order in Wikipedia, in parenthesis, it says conspiracy theory, but on the other hand, there are quite a few videos from many politicians around the world insisting that we need a new world order. The 2030 agenda from the United Nations is basically a new world order. Also, we can observe how underneath the pyramid on the one-dollar bill says Novus Ordo Seclorum, which means a "new order of the ages "that basically means New World Order. To believe in conspiracy theories is like a stereotype. It is supposed to be incorrect, and we can even feel the rejection from people for believing in conspiracy theories or see people who are afraid to accept facts that are not considered official. Is quite common that many people prefer not to believe in conspiracy theories to avoid conflicts because our nature is to be unified. They prefer to follow the official version and stay in their comfort zone, which eventually is not that comfortable. It is always going to be a conspiracy theory if you don't investigate and use your logic and common sense. In a planet rule by lies, the truth is a conspiracy theory, and the ones who believe in conspiracy theories are insane.

We also can observe how the mass media demonizes any unofficial information that does not adjust with them. You need to observe how they are constantly sending you the message that you cannot believe it if is not official. Is obvious that something wrong is happening in front of us. Is time to be aware of how distracted humanity is, following a hidden agenda that is very harmful for all of us, and everyday people are more distracted. Year 2020 marks the beginning of the awakening process that started in 2012, and is also good to know that we are entering the era of Aquarius. It is the end of the age of Pisces, the age of the emotions and beliefs where people have been controlled by the emotion of fear? But the good thing is that as we enter the age of Aquarius, we will experience a massive awakening in humanity. The age of Aquarius is the age of the global mental connection, is the time to embrace and develop those internal gifts that we all possess but are inhibited by the global agenda always interfering in our connection with the divine source. Is the moment of understanding, the moment where the truth is coming out. We are living advantageous moments to improve our lives, but we need to do our job, like developing new creative habits and get out of the destructive ones. You need to get rid of old, useless beliefs. Understand how you have been mentally affected to believe in a distorted reality that deviates you from a better reality. Each one of us creates our reality and as a collective mind, we are creating a global reality that few people want.

Probably one of the biggest mistakes among people is the ambition or need to accomplish society's standards like being obedient, study, get a job, get married, have children, have a house etc., and of course teaching your children the same limiting beliefs you learn. All these behaviors are unconscious and our focus is on achieving our goals, not on self-observation, emotions and feelings, which are constantly creating our reality. Following what has been established by the world institutions is not the best idea. What we need to follow is our heart, our inner voice, these can be powerful if we create a state of balance between our emotions and actions. How many times do we pause and think about ourselves and wonder how we can become a better person? Most people live in a trance without realizing what they are really doing with their life. We always think that we are doing the right things, maybe because we follow most people's patterns without paying attention to the end results.Unfortunately we will find out how we did it when we get old. For some reason, we always think that negative situations happened to other people, not to ourselves. Also, people have the idea that things happen accidentally, but there are no accidents. They are the effect or consequences of our physical and mental behaviors.

Being responsible for any situation that comes to our lives is an act of courage that will help us avoid future inconveniences and, at the same time, help us balance our lives. Have you asked to yourself why, after the age of 50's, so many people start going down instead of having a better life? Look how most people are going in the same direction; we can observe an alarming rate of people in deterioration, and the worst is that people accepted it as something normal. This situation is due to all the programs in our subconscious mind, programs that are designed to keep humanity under control and enrich the powerful ones, among other things.

Many times, you don't need so much evidence to know what's happening on the planet. You just need to take some time and analyze with a rational mind and ask to yourself if is worth it to struggle all your life and end up living in pain and scarcity? Logic and common sense protect us from ignorance. We are living in a society that is in mental decadence. Questioning is a prime element in awareness, and spending some time researching is an act of responsibility towards yourself. Investigate and develop the ability to think without limitations. If you want to decrease your physical effort, you must work with your mental development.

How much time you have spent researching about the origin of your beliefs and who established them? Everybody wants to be a good human being, but not everybody practices the things they need to practice to create the life that we all deserve. Many times, we need to follow our gut feeling and have the willpower to brake with common patterns that the only thing they do is keep us in vicious circles that deteriorate our lives. We need to follow our instincts and our heart and never expect other people's approval, maybe the things we want to do nobody has done it before, so don't expect support or understanding from others. Human beings need to feel accepted by society, and it is easier to think like everybody else, than going against the flow of what has been established. Human beings need to sense that they belong to the herd, rather than feel rejected by society which does not feel good. You need to understand that when everybody thinks the same way, it means that nobody is thinking. They are just following what they have been told without curiosity. One of the consequences of this unconscious behavior is that we are passing our power to others and losing our potential. As a result, most people end up living their lives with frustrations, creating a low vibration in their physical body, leading to all kinds of illnesses. Frustration is the inability to perform and avoid them through execution. I'm not afraid to say that most diseases originate from negative emotions like frustrations, and many of these frustrations are imprinted in your subconscious mind therefore, we're not aware.

If we don't work to get rid of them and we will carry with the situation for the rest of our life. The same happened with wounds from the past, unnecessary guilt complexes, and resentments with other people and with us. All these emotions decrease our energy vibration, and this vibration is what creates our life. Understanding energy is the real journey, where our experiences can be extraordinary. Understanding energy is understanding our essence from where everything is created. Humanity is facing drastic changes; that will provoke confusion and mental chaos, and we need to be prepared. All we need is within us and is waiting for us to be activated, everything starts in our mind with a thought.

Thoughts

Every thought is an energy field and creates a deep interaction with the rest of the Universe. They are channels of communication between your conscious mind and your higher self. When we fixate upon and idea, we nourish it with our attention but also produce a deep connection with its energy or essence, and it manifest in our perception or experience. Therefore, putting our attention on things that empower ourselves can be the best alternative. Thoughts are signals that we send to the Universe, and they are building blocks of our reality. They carry energy with a particular vibration and a specific frequency. These waves of our thought move in all directions, and these waves of frequency will react to waves of similar frequency, attracting and manifesting based upon the levels of our frequency. Thoughts of love, compassion or gratitude are thoughts of high frequencies; on the other hand fear, guilt, regrets, and frustrations carry a low frequency. If we want to have control of what we attract, we need to have control of our thoughts. Good thoughts will enhance the connection with our higher self. The practice of meditation, mindfulness, self-knowledge are the best tools to dominate our thoughts. These practices allow us to access the inner wisdom that guides us in this spiritual journey. Observing our thoughts and analyzing them helps us to understand our values, desires, intentions, and beliefs. We need to quiet our minds and connect with the present moment to enhance our connection with our inner space. Our creative thoughts come from a deep place in our inner being. We intensify our spiritual growth as we get more creative. Also, when we master self-awareness, we can observe which thoughts come from our egoic mind, like doubt, worries and fears or whether they come from our higher self, such as guidance, intuition, love, or compassion. But at the cutting edge, our thoughts, for most part, are influenced by our beliefs and it is a fact that many of these are restraining and detrimental. To eliminate those thoughts that do not serve our wellbeing, we need to eliminate first our limiting beliefs.

Limiting beliefs

Limiting beliefs is a state of mind where your thoughts about yourself restrict your possibilities. These are inner narratives that you have about your life and yourself that hold you back and keep you in constant doubt and fear. They are like imperceptible obstacles preventing us from enjoying our true power. Limiting beliefs are always dampening our confidence, and many of them reside in the subconscious mind constantly affecting our behavior without our conscious awareness. The origin of limiting beliefs can be from past experiences or conditioning from society. It is fundamental to observe and analyze them to determine how rational they are. I want to emphasize again that practices like self-awareness, mindfulness and meditation are probably the best tools to remove your limiting beliefs. Knowing how your mind and brain work is fundamental to figure out how these limiting beliefs were installed in your life and thus being able to eliminate them.

Mind and brain

The mind and the brain are always working together, therefore some basic knowledge about them can be helpful if we want to improve our life. We need to be aware of some basic mechanisms and processes that occur in our brain and our mind because together, they are the command center of our body. We have enough power in ourselves, but is not well developed because we are not aware of all the limitations that we unconsciously accept in our lives. If we want to get out of this collective hypnosis, it is fundamental to understand our brain and our mind and how we have been influenced by depraved programs.

Mind and brain interpret our senses and control our body movements and our behaviors. The most important thing about the mind is that the mind is consciousness, which is everywhere. Probably the whole Universe is a mind, an intelligent magnetic field, the master mind. Our mind is one with the Universe. On the other hand, you have the brain, which, in fact contains large amounts of magnetite, which is a permanently magnetic form of iron oxide, and when studies reveal that brain cells respond to external magnetic fields, we can conclude that probably the magnetite presence in the brain is part of the mechanism that connect our brain with the universal consciousness. In other words, we are all connected to the same magnetic field that you call Consciousness, Universe, or God.

The brain has different vibrational states called brainwaves, and there are five different categories: Gamma with the highest frequencies that oscillate between 38 to 100 HZ related to rapid information processing. They are highly active when we experience love, altruism, also creates cognitive coherence. It is considered the optimal state for functioning. Beta is the dominant state of alert when you are engaged in activities like a conversation, writing, or any other task (12 to 38 HZ). Prolonging in this state is associated with stress, tension, and high blood pressure. Alpha state is a relaxing or meditative state (8 to 12HZ) that promotes creativity and problem solving and allows balanced emotions.

When you are in the alpha state, you can access your subconscious mind, and this fact is important if you want to improve your life. Being in the alpha state boosts your immune system. Meditation is the practice to access this brainwave. Theta waves occur when you are sleeping or in deep meditation. (3 to 8HZ) Theta is associated with intuition, healing, creativity and improving spiritual awareness. Delta waves are created in deep, dreamless sleep and in the deepest meditations (.5 to .03HZ). It is associated with the release of anti-aging hormones and decreases cortisol, the stress hormone that promotes health issues and aging. Knowing this, we can prioritize working with our states of mind and use tools like meditation, aromatherapy and healing sounds that will help to get in the desired brain wave. Learning how to work with our different brain waves is a powerful tool, giving us the opportunity to enhance our productivity or change habits to improve our well-being. This is possible for all of us if we start prioritizing habits, putting more attention on our daily routine and reevaluating our limiting beliefs.

Many of your limiting beliefs were induced by the emotion of fear, and they are imprinted in our **limbic system,** which is the most primitive part of the brain and deals with emotions. It is not well developed during our childhood but is a dominant part of the brain during that period. When we receive information, we do it through the limbic system. It is good to know that most of the time, our traditional beliefs that are learned during childhood are mainly induced by the emotion of fear. At the age of 25 years, when the prefrontal cortex, which is part of the brain in charge of analysis and logic, is well developed, we are so distracted working to accomplish all the things established by society that we never get time to reevaluate those limiting beliefs. The **limbic system** is also well developed at age 25 years and still plays an important role in our lives, and studies show that you receive information through the cerebral cortex, which is connected to the limbic system. The limbic system regulates our emotions and memory. It also deals with learning and sexual lstimulation. Many movements on the planet that promote separation appeal to our emotions, and we support them, understanding that we are doing the right thing. Reevaluate your beliefs; many of them affect your behavior and your expectations.

Our system is always creating fanatics, and the process of becoming fanatic is based on emotions because when we are in emotional states, we are susceptible to acting without thinking, and we are away from logic and common sense. It is time to open our eyes and understand that we have been transferring many limiting beliefs from generation to generation with the idea that someday things are going to get better. But you just need to look around and observe how things are just getting worse, and the only reason is that this has been a design since the beginning of time. This is the moment where you need to wonder about any belief. When you understand that your brain always tries to convince itself of the most comfortable option that best matches its reality, you can understand that it is easier for people to believe in what everybody else belief without creating conflicts, and in the end, most people pay the consequences for accepting ideas without questioning.

In the brain, we also have **mirror neurons**, which are part of the empathy mechanism. They constantly react to what we are observing. The basic example is when we meet somebody, and we have a good connection with that person, unconsciously, we imitate the expressions or movements of the other person. Is very logical to say that this type of neuron is connected to the subconscious mind as well. This means that unconsciously, we are acting like everybody else. Some people say that you are the average of the five people you spend the most time with. Evaluate all your relationships and analyze how every person in your life affects you. This can be hard to accept, but throughout our lives, we must leave behind many people that we love but are not doing any good to ourselves. People do almost everything according to patterns, the tendency is to copy those patterns from other people. To do things according to patterns is natural and can be seen everywhere in the Universe.

When the same information is repeated many times, our neurons start to repeat the same pattern that eventually creates a permanent connection, which is called a **neural net**. They become part of our entity. We have a neural net for each habit and belief that we have. We can rewire all those patterns of limitation in the same way we created them by repetition and exposing ourselves to new ideas and concepts that are beneficial for us. We need to explore and analyze what kind of patterns we are following to have the ability to modify. We need to replace negative thoughts, be honest and take more care of ourselves. Learning to use our mind to our advantage and acknowledging those negative patterns that we acquire from other people is a skill to be developed. I want to draw attention to fanatism, which I consider a social enemy where someone is unwilling or unable to accept a differing point of view, which slows down evolution. It makes people less receptive, preventing them from accepting profitable information in general fanatics lack of self-awareness and have a fixed mindset.

Everybody agrees that the mind is very powerful but not many people pay attention to their mind and take the time to understand basic principles about it. Most people are not committed to knowing and understanding their minds, considering that everything in our life will start with a thought, our mind is the foundation of any experience. How much time human beings should spend working and understanding their mind? Are we aware of what kind of information we have been receiving since childhood? We all have been exposed to twisted ideas of how we should be and how we should think. Understanding the mind and recognizing our mental processes is where we should pay more attention. When we direct our mental faculties toward constructive aspects, we improve our existence and elevate our consciousness. According to our mindset, it is our life. Our perception and how we process any external information is a mark to pay attention to. Our perception will be based on the programs that we accepted without any questioning or giving importance to the origin of those programs. Most people understand that they have their own criteria, but I came up with the term **Induced perception**, which I define as any specific information received designed to foment a definitive criterion. I can see many people saying I have my own criteria so secure, but they don't have an idea how we have been programmed to believe in many things that don't make much sense. By the time we start to be aware of our existence, we already have a lot of information within us. As time goes by, we continuously receive information, and most of this information is already designed to create a specific type of human being, one that is obedient, submissive, powerless, and so distracted that they never learn how to activate their inner potential. But the fluidity of our mind allows us to expand our consciousness.

I want to emphasize our mind is consciousness, is information and probably is everywhere. It is not trapped. It is divided between the conscious mind and the subconscious mind. The **conscious mind** is that part of the mind that is fully aware, the one that is always perceiving, is the one that takes control over logical and intellectual processes. It is the active one when we are currently aware of and thinking about it and living in the present moment. Conscious mind is equal to awareness of our internal and external existence and **Self-awareness** is the ability to perceive and understand how we are and why. It is understanding the things that generate who we are as a person, like our beliefs, personality, actions, values, emotions, and thoughts. Being aware of our behavior is the first step in self-development and is the only way to find out who we really are. Being self-aware means that we possess clarity around what we feel and why, and it also brings a better perception of our qualities, limitations, and patterns. Studies reveal that people with higher self-awareness have better and authentic relationships. It also reveals that as we improve our observation and self-awareness, we affect positively certain regions of our brain like the prefrontal cortex that oversees the regulation of emotional behaviors and important decision making, and it is also involved with your logic and common sense. Self-aware people are better leaders. We always think that what we are doing is correct. But I can observe how many people speak with so much "wisdom', but when we see their life is not balanced, they have many problems, health issues, lack of money. All of these are a consequence of not being aware of how their limiting beliefs affect their lives. If our life is not what we want, it means that we are not doing or believing in what we must do, we are not thinking the way we should, and our beliefs, emotions and perceptions might not be the right ones. One of the key points is to work with your inner being, feeding your spirit with good thoughts and high-quality emotions.

On the other hand, the **subconscious mind** plays a significant role when it comes to changing our mindset and improving our lives. The subconscious mind is the part of your mind of which one is not fully aware but influences one's actions and feelings, which is why, most of the time, we don't need to think or analyze what we are going to do. We just react. I like to say that we all have reactive lives. Studies reveal that our life is manifested 95% from our subconscious mind, but I just prefer to say that most of our life is controlled by the subconscious mind. The number can vary from person to person. The subconscious mind is like a huge memory bank; it permanently stores all kinds of things that we ever experienced. It can remember faces, scents, skills and any kind of events, negative or positive.. Its function is to store and retrieve data and ensure that we respond exactly the way we are programmed.And many of these programs are imposed by the institutions of the planet and their role is not exactly to empower human beings. Our subconscious mind is subjective. It does not reason or think independently; it merely obeys the commands it receives from our conscious mind. Do not do any creative thinking. It cannot distinguish between what is imaginary and what is real. Any thought we repeat over and over or any visual image we create and hold in our mind over and over are examples of the operating system that programs our subconscious mind. An important fact is that our subconscious mind has something called homeostatic impulse, which regulates functions like body temperature, heartbeats and breathing, which means that there is a high possibility that many health issues have their origin in the subconscious mind due to the information that resides in it. This information could be wounds from past experiences, frustrations, guiltiness which are negative emotions that inadvertently affect your physical body. Now understanding the importance of our subconscious mind, we can prioritize to start reprogramming it and unblocking your personal limitations.

Now analyze, if our life is manifested from our subconscious mind where we already have many limiting beliefs, plus we are not aware, it means that most of the time we are creating our life unconsciously. Working with our mental limitations that reside in our subconscious mind is a priority. If our life is not what we want, it is because of existing mental limitations due to programs in our subconscious mind. Therefore, all beliefs should be reevaluated and analyzed if we want to start reprograming our subconscious mind.

The subconscious mind is also the emotional mind, from where our emotion emerges, and these emotions are also based on the existing subconscious mind programs, which are constantly processing and influencing our thoughts and behavior. I must emphasize that most of our thoughts are unconscious and do not align with the things that we want. This is why many times people ask themselves why this happened to them. But never find the answer, because the tendency is to look for the answers in the outer world. Most of the time, we cannot find the right causes of our problems because we are not aware of the invasive programs that reside in our subconscious mind. Digging and understanding our subconscious is probably the best option to understand our life. Therefore, reevaluating those limiting beliefs that hold us back and reprogram our subconscious mind with adequate concepts and ideas is when we open ourselves to the field of infinite possibilities. The subconscious mind is a focal point in our transformation process. Probably, the first step to reprogram our subconscious mind is observing our inner conversation, especially especially what we say about ourselves and about our life because any thought that we repeat over and over is programming our subconscious mind. We basically have the same conversation with ourselves day after day. Being aware of our inner narrative as much as possible is a requirement because that inner conversation is based on the external information that we have been constantly receiving since we were born. This information is constantly programming your subconscious mind and is not align with our true being. Most of the time, we repeat the same negative thoughts over and over, day by day. We are steadily programming our subconscious mind with information that is not constructive for our life. A good practice to reprogram our subconscious mind is when we are falling asleep and when we are waking. Those are the moments where the communication between the conscious mind and the subconscious mind is accessible, it is the moment where we can consciously send positive thoughts directly to the subconscious mind, those moments are the best to visualize and think about your desires. The subconscious mind is programmed by repetition, and we need to develop **mental discipline** to practice affirmations all day long instead of worrying or thinking about things that we don't want.

I define **mental discipline** as the practice of confident thinking, where we think about the things that we want, not about the things that we don't want. It is when we consciously decide to have correct thoughts until they predominate in our mind. It is a consistent engagement in observing our mental processes as much as we can so we can observe our real selves and make the mental adjustments that eventually will create the life that we all deserve. It is the ability to be aware of when we are not thinking correctly and have the capacity to change immediately to the appropriate thoughts, always avoiding doubts and insecurities. We suffer more from the stories that we put in our minds than from the eventual reality, and reality is not just a physical phenomenon but also a mental one. **Mental discipline** is when we are engaged in healthy mental practices that help us to live calmer, with positive emotions, confidence and fewer worries. We need to become another person with a different way of thinking and, therefore with high-quality thoughts and emotions, which are the ones that will shape the life that we want. Like any other discipline, it requires lots of practice. Any life transformation requires discipline.

Another recommended practice is **mindfulness** which is the skill of self-observation in the present moment, acknowledging what we are feeling without judging the emotions or sensations as we feel them, helping us drown ourselves in the now .It is to live in the present moment without the negatives of the past or the worries of the future. **Mindfulness** is one of the tools that we need to use to develop mental discipline. Mindfulness is when we are aware and focus on our feelings and emotions without any reproval about ourselves. It is the ability to live continually observing our intentions, emotions, habits and even our behavior. It is when we develop the skill to live in the present moment using our senses, focusing on sights, sounds, smells, and even textures. Concentrate on what is happening now and accept ourselves without any judgment. We can use breath techniques and pay attention when we inhale and exhale. Practicing **mindfulness** supports good mental health, better stress and anxiety management. Mindfulness also promotes the activation of the prefrontal region of the brain, which is associated with self-control and conscious decision making. The habit **of mindfulness** is the basis for our personal immersion. Whatever we want to develop in our life, whether personal, relationships, professional or spiritual, the habit of **mindfulness** must be present. Keep always in mind that our subconscious mind influences our behavior steadily. Therefore, being mindful is a must. **Mindfulness** is a relationship with the present moment, permitting a sense of clarity and purpose. Paying attention to our actions is what permits us to make changes that lead to a superior vibration. Being mindful amplifies the forces that envelop and surround us, and we must be present to embody a different state of consciousness that will allow us to access enlightenment.

Be aware of those unconscious thoughts that bring undesirable outcomes. Conscious self-observation is the key to breaking those negative patterns that avoid any positive shift in our lives. Any recurrent thought will eventually gain power over us. We need to decide what kind of thoughts are going to be predominant in our mind and choose the ones that build up well-being and fulfillment. When we transform our reality, we also transform the world around us in significant ways.

Being aware of our desires is necessary since they are the reflection of who we are inside; they are a powerful capacity that keep us motivated. Desires are connected to our intentions and is crucial to ensure that those desires come from good intentions to warrant a good outcome. Our desires should come from the intention of advancement, self-improvement and love for ourselves and others.

Change begins from within and is a journey that requires self-exploration of what we really are. Allowing ourselves to see beyond the darkness of our limiting beliefs and identifying patterns that arise from past experiences especially from our childhood ,and self-exploration are practices to follow that will guarantee life transformation. Paying attention to what is brewing in our mind will help to expand our consciousness which leads to get closer to a field of infinite opportunities. When we master our self-observation, we increase our receptivity and our potential to change old unnecessary patterns. Working and understanding our mind is a crucial aspectof our transformation journey. But also understanding how our mind has been influenced by the regime is important as well.

We all make a big mistakes, but one of the most common mistakes is live our life believing in everything we have been told without questioning or investigating. Not many people ask questions, they prefer to give their opinions, which, most of the time are based in little and twisted information. We need to understand that many things that we hear throughout life and constantly repeat them believing they are correct, it could be a mistake. Is time to run our life more logically. Many things that we do every day like taking decisions, purchases, and beliefs we accept, are based on emotions. Remember that emotions play an important role in how our life is manifested, and these emotions are also stored in our subconscious mind and this one has been exposed to many negative external programs.

Most people have not heard the term **psychological subversion** or ideological subversion, which is a strategy developed by the CIA or the KGB in Russia. The main goal of this technique is mind control. These agencies have always been doing experiments with people's minds. Many times the experiments were conducted with military volunteers, and these did not have any idea what they were letting themselves in for. Through psychological subversion, they demoralize people, making them feel powerless. This process also distances human beings from reality. Creating people that prefer to be right before understanding or knowing the truth decreases their receptivity to the point where you can show them logical facts and they will not be able to accept or understand what is reasonable. This mental reaction occurs because of the intentional mind programming that enhances some psychological mechanisms like the **confirmation bias,** which is a mental mechanism that rejects any idea that is not aligned with someone's beliefs or convictions. It is a tendency to search, interpret and recall information in a way that aligns with our pre-existing values, opinions, or beliefs. We always prefer to recognize information that best matches and amplifies what we already believe. A good example is when we say something and the receptor blocks the information, usually changing the topic. If we observe this is a common behavior among many people. We need to be extremely careful about any belief or conviction and our reactions when we are exposed to contradictory information.

I should say it again, we always have been deviated from the knowledge that can be beneficial to us. This mental control is probably one of the biggest obstacles in our society, where people do not have any idea of what they have been exposed to. Mental programming is a very gradual process; therefore, people do not realize the transition. Observe how the operating space has the potential to induce society to accept things that we never imagined. A clear example is what happened during 2020 when the whole world was basically locked down. We have enough power in ourselves, but it is not well developed because we are not aware of all the limitations that we unconsciously accept throughout our lives. If we want to get out of this collective hypnosis, it is fundamental to understand how we have been influenced by depraved programs stored in our subconscious mind that provoke negative outcomes. We need to analyze why, in this world, the emotion of fear is so common and not the emotion of love? My answer is that is part of a design for ‚humanity's control.

We need to look for answers using alternative media, not mass media. This is a moment of awakening where we must believe in our mental and analytical power to discover new horizons where we can enjoy a higher quality of life. We tend to observe other people's behaviors and sometimes criticize them, but the reality is that we all can have the same bad behaviors unconsciously. When we hear about negative human behaviors or people's bad attitudes, instead of pointing out and blaming people, we should decide to think that there could be countless possibilities that we might have the same problem. We are all receiving the same information constantly to think and behave in certain ways, also because we are probably coping other people's behaviors unconsciously due to the existence of the **mirror neurons.** We need to be aware that in the process of being empathic, we can adopt destructive behaviors unconsciously. I am very concerned with the habit of lying, which, of course, must be very usual on this planet due to a system based on lies and an appetite for power. Many times, we lie because we don't want to hurt others or we want to look good, but the problem is that we get used to lying, then we lie unconsciously, and eventually, we also lie to ourselves, affecting different areas of our life. Every time we lie we are sending interfere to our reality, especially when we lie regarding important things. Which is not the same when we lie for compassion. I already have seen many people who spent their lives lying to themselves in many aspects, and in the end, they never get the life they expected. We all need to get out of so many distractions and start practicing self-observation because we all have some degree of negative attitudes, some people more, some people less, but nobody is exempt of it. We can be unconscious in many aspects, for example, when you honk the horn with anger, or when somebody needs help and you don't react, or receive good service in a restaurant and don't leave a tip, when we forget to thank or when you leave a text conversation without an end. All these can happen just because of lack of **self-awareness**. We also can be unconsciously stubborn, close minded, naive and many other things that are not align with the person that we want to be. Everybody likes to feel helpful and be a good human being, but distractions foment unconsciousness. When you are conscious, you are more connected to your inner being and others. Work with yourself because your external world is the echo of your internal world.

You can improve your life basically effortlessly and without pressure or anxiety if you have the right knowledge and practice. This is about us, and we are the most important people in our lives. We are the center of our life and the ones who create it. We continually create our lives based on our emotions, thoughts, feelings, and actions. The number one priority is us. Being distracted with so much useless information is just an intrusion in our transformation process. It is crucial to be cautious and conscious about what we believe and thus be able to adjust our physical and mental behaviors.

When we consider that we learn many things by repetition, it is fundamental to reevaluate any belief that might be affecting our life. We probably have been living without any curiosity about many important topics due to the strong influence of the mass media, where they establish what is popular and what is not. All institutions on this planet are connected and on the same wavelength, working together to keep humanity distracted, segregated,, and demoralized. On this planet, we have all the resources and knowledge to be living in unity, health, and abundance. Everything on this planet is a design, using social engineering since the beginning of time for people control and use some of the same strategies over and over. Many conspiracy theories will stop being theories when people get out of the distractions and start researching and connecting the dots. This is extremely important because before you support something, you really need to investigate to understand what kind of movement you are really supporting. It is a movement that unites people or one that segregates?A movement that is creating chaos or is a movement that is spreading peace and unity? Any organization or institution holds a specific energy vibration, thus, if you are supporting them, you are connecting with their energy, and hence the outcomes related to that energy vibration. For example, Black Lives Matter is a terrorist group that created a lot of separation and destruction, causing approximately 2 billion dollars in losses during the 2020 riots. Abortion movements also carry a low frequency because it is not just the abortion, is what those clinics do with the fetuses, that by the way they call them the product. We should ask to ourselves if we want to be connected to this type of movements that carry such a low vibration. But there are also many other foundations in this world with a double face and a dark agenda behind the scenes. To be aware should be the greatest movement on the planet, the movement that will liberate humanity from this constant chaos. For some people, it is probably hard to understand but we just need to start observing with curiosity and the desire to understand what is going on planet Earth.It is good to take time to investigate because during the investigation process, we attract information that brings a better understanding of our life. You have no idea how good it could be for your existence. Another thing that we must pay attention to is what I already mentioned the **confirmation bias** which is like a germ in our brain that rejects anything that goes against our convictions. Pretty much like the **cognitive dissonance** defined as the discomfort that you feel when you are between conflictive beliefs. (A cognition is a piece of knowledge like a thought, an attitude, a personal value, or behavior). You need to be aware of countless situations where you are affected by the cognitive dissonance. For example, when you are overweight and you have an unhealthy diet, but you want to lose weight, it creates mental discomfort and lowers your frequency, or when you know that you need to quit smoking and you are still doing it, or when we denial the doctrines of religions. Even regrets of past and bad decisions provoke cognitive dissonance. We need to reduce our levels of cognitive dissonance by reevaluating our beliefs or investigating more about the topics that are causing it because **cognitive dissonance,** as the confirmation bias creates bad feelings that alter our emotional states. The confirmation bias and the cognitive dissonance interfere with your receptivity, constantly provoking a stubborn personality. I must keep emphasizing the fact of how we have been programmed and by whom. This is the time to start putting all the pieces together and pursue the truth. Ask yourself, why have there always been secret societies, or governments and institutions like the Vatican with top secrets? In a relationship where there are secrets, it is obvious that there is no sincerity. Lack of honesty predominates on our planet; please be aware, analyze everything and avoid being part of the problem. The argument for keeping top secrets is the reaction of humanity, it is clear that the regime does not want to see the reaction of humanity if they know the truth, many institutions might collapse. I dare say that humanity is prepared to create the world that we all deserve; we just need an opportunity to create another reality. Most people's mindset can be improved if we all create awareness about the established dogmas that affect our lives constantly, intentionally designed by the same institutions, always trying to keep humanity under ignorance. The leaders of the planet have all the knowledge to program the population very smoothly and it has been like this since the beginning of time. They understand perfectly how the brain and the mind work including our subconscious mind, they also know the basic principles of the Universe and how it relates to us and use strategies like social engineering to regulate and change the development and behavior of society. But now is the time where we all can learn the basic concepts to shape the life we expect. We have been programmed to believe that we are powerless and defend the official version only, where they are always sending the message to the public "do not believe in anything if is not officialized" in other words, don't investigate, don't jump out of the box. Remember how being obedient was such a big issue in our childhood, and how they punish us if we were wrong, as a result most people are afraid of being against what has been establish or being wrong, becoming stubborn people that unconsciously avoid any information that is not officialized, with the certainty that they are right when is probably the opposite. My observation is that this type of person does not have the life they really want. Another fact is when we analyze the prevailing message of being a good citizen, which implies being obedient and do whatever they ask you to do. The best example was, during 2020 one of the big issues was get the vaccine, and eventually many people are having health issues after they got vaccinated, beside all the people that die after getting it including many young athletes. I suggest that we all should start reevaluating all the things that we support blindly, without any investigation. At the age of 66 I already have seen many people's lives, since they were young, and I don't like what I observe. I remember seeing friends and family how most of them live their lives, motivated, with curiosity and ambitions, but at one point they start losing their logic and common sense and hence their reasoning, brightness, and motivation, and all of them with the common factor of being very loyal to the system and the official statement. I observe how they got more fearful, less enthusiastic, and of course extremely stubborn. I also can see and understand how everybody wants to be a good human being and do things correctly, but their lives are not what they want, is obvious that something is not working out. I must emphasize; reevaluate your beliefs and your priorities. What is happening that you see so many people struggling with health and personal issues most of their life? Any significant change in your life will come true when you change all those settled programs of fears, separation, submission and impotence.Is time to acknowledge that humanity has been induced to lose their logic and common sense and follow and support a negative agenda. We need to concentrate on ourselves and understand the categories of distractions like job, family, friends, and electronic devices. Then decide how you are going to prioritize your daily life, to give way to the life that you want. We need people that live their lives with more curiosity, people that ask questions, people that are less distracted and truth seekers.

CHAPTER 3

In my personal process I have learned that we need to answer many questions about our existence, there upon is required to get out of the useless distractions and investigate more about everything. If we really want to improve our life we need to have a broad idea of the mechanisms of life, like understanding our mind and body, developing better social skill, understand basic principles of finances, understand how governments and institutions of the planet really works and the most important, understand the mechanism that move our spirit. Having a good job does not guarantee a good life.We need to live our lives with curiosity and consciousness because most of the time we are reacting based in the preexisting programs imprinted in our subconscious mind. Everyone thinks that what they are doing is correct, but unfortunately will know how good or bad we did at the end of our lives. This is the moment to make decisions that uplift our life, make decisions that have results in the long term. Instant gratification and shortcuts are not the best options, personal transformation is a slow process that requires a lot of self-observation and eventually brings a lot of satisfaction.

CHAPTER 4

In the book "The MasterKeySystem" from Charles Haanel, a book that was forbidden when it came out in 1912, I read quite a few times throughout the book" Your external world is a manifestation of your internal world", since that moment I decided to start working more with myself, and the first step was to get out of so many distractions. But immediately I asked myself, what is my inner world, eventually I understood, that our inner world are all those mental processes that we have in a daily basis, like your thoughts, emotions, feelings, perceptions, and beliefs. Being aware of our mental processes is the key for life improvement because most of this need constant adjustment due to their origin. Since our childhood we start learning many things and we follow them without asking and believing that everything we have been taught is correct. This is the moment where humanity needs to start believing more in themselves and activate their prefrontal cortex to analyze facts and events that are constantly telling us that many things we have been taught are not correct.

Reasoning is part of our internal world, lately I have been observing how many people fail this skill, eventually it came to my mind the term **rational intelligence** which can be define it as the ability to collect and analyzed information and eventually have an assertive conclusion, especially when that conclusion could be very profitable and constructive to ourselves. Some examples about lack of rational intelligence are: When I hear people saying the News are constantly lying " but their criteria is based on what they see in the News, or I don't like the war but support the leaders that love to kill people in war, or when people say " I believe in God, but I don't believe in religions, which does not make much sense because religions are the only ones that promote God existence. All these behaviors are totally unconscious. Most people don't have an idea of how unconscious we can be.Many times, we accept ideas and concepts automatically without analyzing them, rather we accept them driven by empathy or understanding that if the majority accepts it, it is correct.

Our brain is unable to recognize if the information is true or false, and even more when we learn many things by repetition. We probably have been living without any curiosity about what is going on in this Planet where there is so much knowledge and technology and things are getting worse. We have all the resources and knowledge to be living in unity, health, and abundance, then why there is always a conflict and decadence? We are living in moments where people need to be more conscious about their surroundings, behaviors and beliefs. I observe the levels of unconsciousness among people, where they want to improve their lives, but they are unaware of how they really are. Being open minded is a great asset where we are willing to accept our wrongness, new ideas and changes, but unfortunately many people are unconscious about their behavior and reactions. It is like a virus spreading throughout the world supported by peoples denial. I decided to create a term to describe this state of mind where people are unconsciously decreasing the capacity to accept new ideas and concepts.

If you want to solve a problem you need to make a diagnosis first. I decided to create the terminology **Fixable Unconscious Reception Impairment (FURI)** which is the inability to accept new ideas or concepts, maybe it can be categorized as another cognitive bias. You can understand clearly that is a **reception impediment** that makes people less interested in certain topics, and sometimes these topics are helpful to improve their lives. Being open-minded goes beyond saying I'm open minded, it is to have the capacity to listen with the desire to understand. Most minds are designed to get ready to shoot back rather than listen with empathy and appreciation. Being open-minded is also to be willing to investigate.

It is **unconscious** because we are not aware that we all have it, (different people different levels), commonly the older the person the higher their levels of this reception impairment. The main problem resides in the subconscious mind where you have stored all those limiting beliefs and programs that you have learned during your life and these programs and beliefs are avoiding and interfering with your reception. Everybody thinks they have an open mind, because most human beings are not aware of how they really are. Anybody can get rid of any limiting belief when you understand and accept that you are living in a twisted reality. Putting enough interest in the process of becoming more receptive and always been aware that the problem is unconscious is fundamental to start opening your mind or in better words opening your consciousness.

It is **fixable** because our brain has neuroplasticity which is known as the ability of neural networks in the brain to change through growth and reorganization, it is the potential to change patterns at a neural net level. We all have different neural nets for every belief or habit. You can reset any patterns, beliefs, and convictions and rewire your brain as needed, especially when it is a matter of self-improvement. Understanding the ability to fix most situations in our life is part of our mindset, always creating empowering habits and paying attention to those habits that are the result of the inability to accept new ideas or concepts.

Behaviors associated with the FURI, like obstinacy and the desire to be always right bring unhealthy relationships, frustration, isolation, depression, and anxiety, and these are inhibitors of your spiritual growth. Being receptive places you in a perpetual state of learning, bringing information to deal with your perception of inability to perform. Being more receptive leads to having better interaction with others and manage your thoughts and emotions properly. Embrace the convenient skills of being receptive to always learning new things and observing how your life starts flourishing. Another behavior associated with the FURI is the"I know"response, but if we think that we know, we never have the opportunity to learn new things, which is like closing the door to knowledge.

Many times, we all have a wrong perception of who we really are, considering that our subconscious mind is constantly absorbing information from outside sources and using that information to form beliefs that affect the way you think and behave. It is crucial to pay attention to any kind of external information and always wonder how that information can affect our habits and behaviors. It is fundamental to be mindful of any kind of information, especially when it comes from any recognized institutions or organizations. The entertainment industry creates fanatics and distracts people from matters of greater importance, having, as a result, unaware personalities that spend their whole life looking for instant gratification and acceptance. We are all victims of mental control, but you don't need to feel like a victim. You just need to be aware of the situation and look beyond the official statement. It is not a problem to accept that we have been wrong, the problem is when you don't accept it and remain clinging to obsolete paradigms, which have no benefits for your life.

You can change the way you think without feeling guilty about not being aligned with the society's standards; unfollow the crowd, be yourself and have a passionate intention to transform your existence. We all love to look like we know, but it is more important to pretend that we don't know. This attitude triggers curiosity and the desire to investigate or ask, which is probably a fundamental step to start opening our consciousness. Paying attention to our subconscious behaviors is fundamental for our wellbeing. We don't need to know everything. What we need to know is that most of the time, we are not conscious of what we say or how we behave because we are reacting according to the programs in our subconscious mind. It is time to ask ourselves why many people spend their whole lives struggling to achieve what they are supposed to achieve and eventually end up living in scarcity and lack of health? One of the answers could be because most people get stuck with the same old ideas and concepts and never observe their behaviors. Besides, they love to follow the official version that is is designed to destroy people's minds and lives. Observe and analyze why, as people grow up and get older, they are more stubborn. Maybe it is time to be more aware of what kind of information we are receiving that turns most people so rigid.

I grew up around well-educated people (of course, with all their limiting beliefs), people who consider education as a priority, people who gave me advice when I needed guidance, but eventually, they got to some point where they stayed believing in the same limiting beliefs and getting less receptive. Unfortunately, the common behavior is that they prefer to be right instead of having the courage to listen and try to understand and pursue the truth. At some point,, we all must face this type of situation, and we must deal with mental rigidity. Remember those moments when we tried to make our elders understand new ideas, and it was impossible to make them understand, if we don't pay attention someday, we unconsciously can be doing the same thing. Be aware that as we get older, there is a high probability of being stubborn as well. By experience and observation, being stubborn is one of the causes of suffering and depression. We need to make a commitment to reach old age with a receptive mind and do not make the mistake of thinking that we are receptive or open minded when we are not. I recommend doing a social experiment and ask people of different ages if they are open mind; then, we can see that the answer is always yes. Everybody believe that is open minded because of lack of self-observation. Developing the ability of self-exploration and feed your curiosity are open gates to a meaningful life. We may have heard that knowledge is power, but knowledge is power when we know how to use it and practice what we preach. I observed how I learned many beneficial concepts from some people throughout my life, things that I retain, analyze and practice, but they just have the knowledge but never practice bringing unwanted situation to their lives. I observe how important it is for people to feel that they know and be able to show it. Nobody wants to be wrong, and that is probably due to childhood programming where if you were wrong on a test you were punished with a bad grade and even by our parents. Of course, I'm not blaming anybody. I prefer to spend my energy figuring out what kind of information we are receiving that makes us behave like that, and this is a situation that involves everyone, we just need to be aware of this behavior that affects our reception. Being receptive means that we are willing to receive and receiving knowledge is the most important. This is the era of information; we just need to become more enthusiastic about learning new things and investigate every new tendency. Throughout our lives, we constantly have opportunities to improve ourselves but most people lose them for not being aware of their reception impairment. Being conscious about our behavior might be a hard task to achieve, but it is a requirement for self-improvement.

A lack of self-awareness is like a mental disorder affecting our lives constantly. I want to emphasize how, most of the time, we react without paying attention to our behaviors. We always understand that we are right, but our life indicates how right or wrong we are. If we don't masterself-awareness, we will never have the chance to know who we really are, and we will lose the opportunity to improve ourselves. This is the moment when information is accessible to anyone; we just need to become more enthusiastic about keeping our curiosity active and learning new things. Being receptive or not has to do with our mindset and is always affecting our lives.

Changing our life means changing the way we think and behave. At some point we need to become another person with another way of thinking and behaving, without losing our essence or the real us. That is why the new cliché says, "If you want to change your life, you must change the way you think." in simple words means, you need to change your **mindset**.

Your **mindset** is the sum of your knowledge, perceptions, emotions experiences, beliefs, feelings, and thoughts. It is an established set of attitudes of a person or group regarding values and points of view. Any mental process is related to your **mindset,** also is the perception about the world and us. It determines how we receive and react to information. Our mindset will constantly influence our behavior and outcomes.

We need to examine our beliefs, which are active components in our mindset, and moreover, accept that many beliefs affect our life in a negative way. Also, understand that our limitations come from designed programming with a hidden agenda. It is time to decide if we want to stay supporting a system that promotes human degradation or have the courage to start changing our mental habits and protect ourselves from a corrupt agenda? Past generations have always supported this malevolent system because they did not have access to information like we have today, but now information is accessible and explicit. We just need to be more diligent and receptive and get more time to evaluate the information around us.

Changing our mindset requires us to accept that the way we think needs adjustment. Expanding ourminds to infinite possibilities is an intelligent and advantageous option if we really want to improve our lives. We need to choose courage over fear ,believe in ourselves, and always be willing to take risks. The way we think and interpret our life is based on our belief system which is constantly affecting our emotional states. When we understand that we create our life based on our emotions, actions and perceptions, changing our mindset is a priority. We can make the decision to have courage and go against what has been established or stay in the familiar zone and experience what most people undergo throughout life, but in the end, any decision has a consequence.

When we talk about mindset, it is fundamental to identify the two types of mindset : The first one is **a fixed mindset,** where the person believes the intelligence, skills and personality are fixed traits that cannot be changed or improve. It is when a person understands that their abilities are innate and unchangeable. A fixed mindset leads to people who prefer to stick to what they know instead of trying new things. They feel vulnerable and never make the effort to improve themselves. But also, the fixed mindset gives a sense of belonging where people find their niche in any situation, they conform easily. **Growth mindset** is the universal mindset where we live in the field of possibilities, it is also when we believe that we can improve and grow constantly as a human being. People with a growth mindset have determination and work hard for what they want, they embrace challenges ,are open to learn new things and accepting changes. People with a growth mindset possess high self-awareness always trying to understand themselves to evaluate their skills to gain understanding about their talents. They are good listeners who understand different perspectives. They have emotional resilience and stay driven **from within**. People with a growth mindset have more brain activity than the ones with a fixed mindset. All these assets lead to efficient setting and achieving goals. We can be more specific and think about our mindset associated with money, relationships, and health. For example, when you think about money, what do you think, are you paying attention to your thoughts about money? When you are paying something, do you think I'm running out of money, or money is constantly flowing through me? How many times do you think I cannot afford it, instead of thinking someday I'm going to have it. How is your mindset about relationships? Do you think that you deserve high quality friends and harmonious long-term relationships, or you think that you don't deserve it, or I'm not good enough? The same with your health, do you understand that you are strong and healthy, or do you think that you are powerless and vulnerable to any disease? Everything is about our mindset, what we say about us or about our life is what eventually will come true. It is important to know that our mindset is the result of our beliefs and convictions that settle in our subconscious mind. Doing affirmations as much as we can instead of worrying all the time is a practical way to reprogram your subconscious mind. Change your worries for gratitude. Worrying is like praying for the things that you don't want. Where you put your attention, you are putting your energy into it, and that is what we attract.

If we want to develop a growth mindset, start viewing challenges as opportunities, try different learning sources and tactics, stop seeking approval, embrace the process over the result, replace the word failing with the word learning, and always acknowledge new concepts and ideas, investigate with the intention of understanding and pursue the truth so you can have your own criteria. During the process of changing our mindset, it is important to recognize that fears and the need for approval can restrict our development. Always look for people that are on the path of improving themselves and people that want to grow as well.

We don't need to think like everybody else, where everyone thinks the same way. It means that no one is thinking, and significant changes are impossible.

As soon as we change our priorities and our mindset our life is going to change for the better. We are supposed to be in a constant learning process, constantly asking ourselves, what can I learn? What can I improve? Any situation that comes into our life is to bring some kind of knowledge if we are paying attention. Life is about learning. The more you learn, the more you expand. The brain's neural plasticity gives us the opportunity to change any mental pattern that is not align with our improvement process and always remember to t acknowledge new concepts and ideas.

In our brain, there are neural nets associated with our social and personal behaviors that need to be changed. Neural nets are the foundation of our daily routines, that, most of the time, we do unconsciously. Every time we learn a new thing, we add new connections to our brain, creating new neural pathways. It is always good to step into the unknown and believe in our potential to change anything, and believe in our ability to change any patterns. Being mindful and self-aware is crucial if we want to reprogram our subconscious mind, and being conscious of how we spend our time will accelerate the process of becoming the person that we want.

Once again, I want to emphasize how distractions keep humans disconnected from themselves. Probably one of the most dangerous strategies against humanity of all times is distraction. Observing your thoughts, emotions, feelings, intentions, and perceptions equals to observing our energy vibration, which is the one that determines our life. The attention must be within us, observing ourselves constantly is a skill that we all must develop. When we understand what we are doing and why we are doing it, is when we start having control of our life and start creating the life that we want. To understand the process of changing our mindset, it is important to recognize that fears can restrict our development. Fears are one of the most powerful emotions, and our very survival depends on them, fears are triggered in the limbic system, which is responsible for alerting and protecting ourselves from danger. Our fears also reside in our subconscious mind. We need to be honest with ourselves and acknowledge that there is always something that we need to improve, like managing fears. Tapping in our subconscious mind should be our new habit, considering that it is the best practice to figure out any kind of limitation like our fears, and others induced enslaving beliefs that constantly hold us back. Fears are patterns that your subconscious mind already accepted as facts. Any experience has a huge impact on our subconscious mind, and it could be a series of negative events, imposed beliefs or any traumatic experiences from the past. Throughout the years when coaching employees, I have found people so fearful and stubborn that they cannot even accept that we all have fears interfering in our lives. We need to accept and understand fears, so we can have the understanding to manage them or get rid of them. We need to detect fears and try to figure out their origin, ask ourselves why we have that emotion. The origin of many fears comes from childhood experiences and wounds from the past that we never heal. Fearful people tend to be less proactive and more defensive, even hateful. Understanding and managing our fears is the fastest way to get rid of them. Also, we need to understand that sometimes making decisions under fear can lead to negative results. On the other hand sometimes you must do certain things although you are in fear and in the end, we can realize that they were just a creation of our minds.

Fears will always be part of our lives, and we must commit ourselves to being aware how we react. We all can have moments where we are not aware of our reactions, and we already know that our life is manifested in a high percentage based on what you carry in the subconscious mind; this also means that most of the time, we are reacting, without paying attention to our actions, feelings, and emotions. This is what I like to call "reactive living." The goal is to move ourselves to a state of awareness where o we recognize the things we need to fix. One of the things that we all must fix is when we face situations against our beliefs, and we react by arguing back instead of asking. It is important to keep in mind that there is a high probability of not having enough or the right information in our hands? Our planet is a sea of lies, creating confusion steadily, where many people are convinced of what they are saying and unaware that they are just repeating what they have been listening all their life without any analysis or investigation. Always remember that history was written by the ones who got control, and they just inform what is convenient for them, and this is totally real. A receptive person should ask before shooting back. For example: I never heard about that, can you explain to me? Why are you saying that? How long have you been researching about it? What kind of sources do you use for your research? When we act like this, we open our minds to the field of possibilities.

Opening our minds to new ideas and concepts is the best way to start a positive transformation process. Spend more time investigating. When we research, we are curious which means that we are being receptive and creating opportunities to discover new things that eventually can be beneficial for us. Many times, people have misconceptions about life due to a lack of information, and create unwanted outcomes. We all love to look like we know, but we don't need to know everything. What we really need is to accept that most of the time, we are pretending that we know just to look good, and, at the same time, losing the ability to be receptive. This common behavior is unconscious and doesn't do any good to us. Be aware of this kind of behavior because it is probably one of the causes why most people spend their whole lives struggling and eventually end up living in scarcity and lack of health. Being receptive is an asset for a better life. Another common mistake that interferes in our reception is when we try to share a personal story with somebody, and as soon as we start, they interrupt to let us know that they have a similar story, putting themselves first and demonstrating no interest in our story. This bad habit also makes people less emphatic and less receptive.

Chapter 5

It is encouraging that our planet is in a process of awakening where neuroscience and quantum physics are bringing enlightenment to everyone. Now, we all can understand the mechanism of how we create our reality where everything starts with the thoughts that spark our feelings and emotions, which are the ones that determine our energy vibration. Vibration is measured in frequencies, and this information is sent to the Universe. In other words, frequencies are the language of the Universe, and our emotions are the language of our body and will dictate most of our lives. Two thousand years ago, Plato talked about the importance of emotions, but of course, any beneficial knowledge was eventually suppressed or put aside. But in 1996, Peter Salovey and John Mayer came up with the term **emotional intelligence**, which was popularized by Dan Goleman in his book of the same name.

Emotional intelligence is the ability to understand emotional responses, manage them and manage other people's emotions. **Emotional Intelligence** enables stronger connections, a more profound understanding of people and it also helps to build up empathy and self-control. One of our goals should be to reach that emotional maturity when we face different opinions or criticism, and we remain calm and receptive, or when in hectic moments we remain composed under pressure rather than reacting with anger or fear. Emotions are energy moving within us, and when we recognize it, we are aware, giving way to have control of them. When we lack awareness, emotions take over, and we lose control of our lives. We need to pay attention to our emotional fields to have control of our inner states. We always need to embrace and analyze emotions, considering that they are steadily configurating our lives. Now that we can recognize how important our emotions are and how they are constantly affecting many areas of our lives, it is good to learn the three components of emotions: the first one is the subjective component, which has to do with how we process our feelings and emotions, the second one is the physiological which has to do with how our body reacts to our feeling and the third is the expressive component and has to do with how to behave when responding to our feelings. If emotions are energy in motion, constantly regulating our energy vibration is essential to be aware of what kind of emotions we carry and what kind of frequencies we generate. It came to my mind that we should have a new concept called **ergon-emotional intelligence**, but before delving into this concept, we must understand some basic principles of energy and the Universe.

Energy

Since we were kids, we have always heard the word spirit, understanding that is something part of us that is also related to God. But it has always been mysterious how this mechanism of spirituality really works, is like buying a car without knowing how to drive it. I can hear people saying I'm spiritual, and I understand what they mean, but everybody is spiritual because we all have a spirit. Being spiritual just does not mean that you pray to a God, meditate, use crystals or burn incense. What I have learned so far is that spirituality is to understand and manage our energy behavior. It is to master the knowledge of how we control our energy vibration. Spirituality also means how our energy is related to the rest of the Universe. We create the life we want if our spirit is vibrating in the right frequency. It is vital to understand that our spirit is that fragment of energy that belongs to our physical body, and it is also connected to the rest of the Universe, where everything is also energy. When we learn the mechanism of our relationship with the Universe, we can say that we have advanced in our spiritual journey. This is the knowledge that will bring more understanding about us and our lives. Talking about energy is not the most appealing topic for many people, although it is a fundamental to understand the process of transformation which is an energetic process.

Energy is the force that moves everything, always vibrating in different frequencies, and reacting with each other. The same applies to our spirit, which is always vibrating and reacting with invisible forces or, in other words, interacting with the energy of the rest of the Universe. It is crucial to understand how our energy behaves or vibrates, that behavior is measured in frequencies, and these are the ones that dictate our life, remember, frequencies are information in terms of the Universe. We have physical energy, which is the quantity of energy; when we exercise, we are generating physical energy. If you don't have a good diet or lack of rest then your physical energy decreases. Then we have emotional energy, being the quality of energy. When we love and enjoy our life, it is a good energy. When you are in fear or feel danger is a low-frequency energy. Another type is mental energy, which is the focus of our energy. While you are doing an important job our energy is centered in our task. And the spiritual energy, the force of your energy, this is the one that determines your feeling, how you feel about yourself, whether you feel confident, powerful or whether you feel doubtful and impotent. Every time we have an emotion, we emit a vibration that is sent to the Universe, and this vibration will interact with similar frequencies. Everything is energy and is all connected, and there is no separation.

The Universe or Your Higher- Self

The infinite magnetic field where we all belong, the mastermind where we all participate, and we are one with the Universe. Everything in the Universe is energy, always in constant motion. It is a pulsating entity that acknowledges and responds to the stream of the human mind. The Universe is constantly perceiving any subtle vibration that emanates from our thoughts, emotions, or feelings. The Universe is a holistic system where everything is connected to the whole. Everything in the Universe is vibrating, including us, and these vibrations have a frequency that affects our whole life, our interactions with others, our health, and our overall life trajectory. Our vibration frequency is like a radio station broadcasting to the Universe; when we are toned at a high vibrational frequency, we attract similar positive energies and experiences. The Universe is in constant expansion and encourages cooperation, and it is a friendly Universe. The Universe extends grace, patience, and infinite possibilities. Therefore, if we are the Universe, we should flow with the rhythm of the Universe. One of the main purposes of this life is to learn how to be aligned with the Universe or our higher self. The term higher self gives us the awareness and the sense of belonging to the magnetic field where everything exists. It is good to mention that our higher self always wants us to be good and is always trying to communicate with us in different ways, like intuition, premonitions, and synchronicities. The Universe will always align in our favor, bringing us everything that resonates with our frequencies. Being aware of what kind of frequencies we are sending to the Universe is a skill that every human being should develop. Physical reality is a projection of the Universe. Understanding the interconnectedness between the physical, spiritual, and emotional dimensions is an essential knowledge that explains how we shape our human reality. These three dimensions are essentially related, conditioning each other in subtle ways. We need to acknowledge this unity that resides within us and is constantly defining our reality. Understanding this concept will help us to figure out what is harmful or beneficial for our spirit. To enhance our connection with our higher self, we need moments of quietness, allowing a better understanding of our soul. It is when we start activating the wisdom that exists in the Universe and resides within us. Understanding the Universe is fundamental for our daily life since we are the Universe. Imagine a cell from our body that we can only see with a sophisticated microscope. That cell has organs and systems, where constantly occur six main functions to keep us alive. Now, observe our body also have organs and systems, and the same thing happens in a larger level. This explains the fractal nature of the Universe, which means the same pattern exists from the micro scale to the macro scale. Realize how the cosmic web looks somewhat like a human brain. Now visualize one cell of our body. That cell is part of us, ,and that cell is ourselves, therefore, in terms of energy, we are like a cell in the Universe. Does not matter what kind of beliefs we have. It is necessary to understand the concepts of the Universe because we are the Universe. The Universe is mental, and we are a fragmented mind from the whole mind. It is necessary to pay more attention to our mental processes these being the ones that define our life.

If every thought triggers an emotion, and when we consider that most of the time, we are unaware of our thoughts, we are at the mercy of our emotions. This incursion in our mind constantly affects our physical and emotional health, triggering unwanted events in our lives. When we silence our mind, we can listen to our inner voice, and mind stillness brings life control. When we live in calm, we are sending a message to the Universe saying that everything is alright. Do not try to change things or people ever. Every time we try to change a situation equals to go against the flow of the Universe. Also when we try to change somebody's behavior or beliefs, we are interfering in their personal process and sending the wrong message to the Universe. Of course, if there is a person who asks you for advice or coaching to improve his life, it is different because it is the person's will, but in general matters, is better to be the observer and keep ourselves in a peaceful state. To learn how to understand our thoughts, emotions, and intensions without reacting and avoid unnecessary stress and anxiety is one of the most important goals in life. Many times, to enjoy quietness, we must let goof old concepts, dogmas, and wounds from the past. Always keep in mind that we are constantly creating our reality, and many times, this process is an unconscious behavior. We create our reality in collaboration with the Universe, but why have we never been encouraged to study and understand how to apply the Principles of the Universe to our life? It is time to empower yourself, time to understand that we are the Universe, and we should learn, understand and practice the principles that govern it.

Universal Principles

As I mentioned before, there has always been information that has not been available to everyone, especially information that is vital for human well-being. But in this friendly Universe, there are laws that affect our lives on a daily basis, and most people ignore them. The hermetic principles provide the knowledge that every human being should know as a child. When we understand these laws, we can understand ourselves and our role in the Universe. These principles are the ones that govern our reality and help us transform our lives and bring a better understanding of many aspects of our lives, and they are guidelines we should follow to improve our existence. These principles will empower any human being, bringing control harmony and amplifying their spiritual and personal growth.

The first principle is **mentalism,** which states that all is mind, the foundation of the universe is consciousness. Everything we see and experience is a manifestation of the divine mind, and we are part of that mind, we are also part of the collective consciousness. Mastering our thoughts is the key to shaping the life that we want. It is important to understand the interconnectedness between the mind and the matter, where our thoughts and consciousness are intricately connected to the physical world around us Everything that we create or achieve begins in our minds. Being abundant, healthy, or happy are all states of mind. All of them depend on the person's mindset. Everything is consciousness, and we are fragments of the same universal consciousness that have split off from the source to undergo different experiences. Mentalism is the melting pot from where the alchemy of creation emerges. We live and move within the mental expression of the Universe. If the mind is the origin of all things, being mindful should be a constant practice.

The second principle is **correspondence**, this principle expresses as above, so below, as within, so without. It means that there is a correspondence or similarity between different levels of existence. The macrocosm (the large) reflects the microcosm (the small). Everything is connected and interrelated in a harmonious way. These are patterns and laws that govern all aspects of reality, from the physical to the spiritual world. What is happening inside of you will be reflected on the outside. Your external reality reflects your internal state. Changing our inner world is the first step to change our outer world. The Universe reflects to us what we project.

Your health is a reflection of your thoughts and emotions about your body, your relationships are a reflection of your thoughts and emotions about yourself and others, and your career is a reflection of your thoughts and emotions about your work and purpose.

The third principle is **vibration,** and says that everything in the Universe moves, nothing rest, everything is vibrating in different levels of frequencies. We are constantly vibrating in different frequencies based in our thoughts and emotions, and these frequencies are continuously affecting our reality. Vibration is mental, spiritual, and emotional in nature. The principle of vibration also confers upon us the ability to influence the vibration of those around us, whether it be for their benefit or detriment. With our positive vibrations, we can inspire and heal others or the opposite. Additionally, we can draw others closer or push them away based on our vibrations, and we will always attract people that have similar frequencies, understanding that frequencies are information. I want to give an example; many times when I have quick encounters with people, I found out that we have things in common, for example, people that are or have been in the restaurant business, people who like water sports like windsurfing the one I practice for many years, also people that like my favorite topics to talk about. I wanted to share this to have a better understanding of how frequencies bring different types of information and how people that you attract can help you to understand how you really are. Of course, when we have encounters with people of negative attitudes, it is probably harder to accept that somehow that person is vibrating in a similar frequency, but those moments are the ones where we have to pay more attention and ask to ourselves why we have the experience. Remember, we need to spend more time figuring out how we really are. I understand that probably our whole energy (spirit) has all types of frequencies happening simultaneously; furthermore, the whole spirit carries the average of all those frequencies as a total frequency. This is the frequency that will determine what you attract. Frequencies can be dissonant or can be resonant, that's why we must be in constant self-observation to develop the ability to adjust our vibration. Resonance and dissonance in our vibrations is a fundamental aspect of the law of attraction, which declare that likes attract like. The more you resonate positively, the more positively it reverberates back. We attract what we are, which is hard to accept for some people, especially when they attract negative events or people. But they must consider their levels of unconsciousness and acknowledge the great opportunity they have to figure out how they really are. The vibration principle brings a great responsibility toward yourself and others. An ancient saying was," He who vibrates with the highest will be the leader of the lowest."

The fourth principle is **polarity,** and declares that everything is dual, everything has poles, and everything has its pairs of opposites that are identical in nature but different in degree. For example, hot and cold and light and darkness are not separate things but different aspects of the same spectrum. It means that you can change your perception of the situation by shifting the polarity. We can choose to see the negative or positive side of anything. This allows us to find a balance between the extremes and tap into the full spectrum of possibilities. Maybe all truths are, but half-truths and all paradoxes may be reconciled. This principle can bring peace of mind when you master how to shift polarities. My favorite example is when I faced negative events and I forced my mind to find out the positive side; I do not always see the positive side show up immediately, but keeping a positive attitude about the situation accelerates the solution.

The fifth principle is **rhythm,** deliver that everything flows in and out, everything has its tides, and all things rise and fall. Everything in the Universe moves in cycles. There are periods of action and rest, of joy and sadness, cycles of the moon, seasons in the year, we live and die. A vital aspect of the rhythm principle is that nothing is ever permanent. Everything has a beginning and end. It is good to clarify that many times, the length of our life cycle depends on our effort or our laziness.

The sixth principle is **cause and effect, which** claim that nothing happens by chance and that everything has its cause. Every cause has its effect, and every effect has its cause. There are no accidents in the Universe. Actions have consequences. Every choice that we make has an effect. Whatever happens there must be a cause for it, nothing comes from nothing. Everything that is happening in the Universe is a chain of causes and effects. This applies to all levels of existence: spiritual, mental, and physical. On the spiritual level, your thoughts and beliefs create your reality. On the mental, your attitudes and emotions influence your actions, and on the physical, your actions produce your results. Your habits, for example, are the repeated actions that you perform every day, consciously or unconsciously, and these are the cause of your outcomes. We are not victims of circumstances. We are creators; we can choose to act in ways that align with our spiritual purpose or waste our time in useless distractions. The goal is to generate good thoughts and emotions and cultivate healthy habits. This principle points to the fact of taking responsibility for your own life rather than blaming others. Everything you do in your day will have an effect, and it will create a ripple of events associated with the nature of your actions. Your thoughts and emotions are the cause of our actual situation. Being responsible starts when we understand and accept this principle.

The seventh principle is the principle of **gender,** revealing that everything has both masculine and feminine aspects of modalities. They are modes of expression that apply to our thoughts and emotions. Masculine energy is active, assertive, logical, rational, analytical and goal oriented. The feminine energy is passive, receptive, intuitive, creative, emotional and process oriented, and these energies are complementary. They work together to create harmony and balance in ourselves and the Universe. We need to balance both energies within ourselves and in our relationships with others. Embrace both energy aspects in your being and do not suppress neither one. Integrate logic and intuition, analysis and creativity, action and reflection and experiment with the wholeness of life. Everything in the Universe is about balance. As human beings, it is our responsibility to look for balance in every aspect of our lives.

Another law that governs our Universe is the **law of the divine oneness**; this law is the foundation for the laws that are included in the hermetic principles. This law lets us understand that we are all connected to the same source of energy. We are all one, I am you, and you are me. We are all divinely inseparable, creating universal consciousness. The vibration of any one of us affects the universal consciousness. We live in a celestial network where everything is united and affecting each other therefore, our spiritual growth is so important considering how we influence the rest of the Universe. If we live in sadness, regrets, and worries, we are sending messages of low frequencies to the Universe. As we grow spiritually, we can raise our frequencies and hence raise the frequency of the planet. I dare to say that raising the frequency of the planet could be a solution to many global problems. We all can make a significant positive impact if we become more aware of what we are feeding to the collective consciousness. I understand that we live in a collective delusion created by all the beliefs and perceptions shared by humanity and passed from generation to generation without questioning or realizing all the limitations that these beliefs carry. The reality that we are living in is a product of our collective consciousness. Embark in the journey of mental transmutation and be part of a positive transformation in the world.

A phenomenal fact about the oneness of the Universe is that if we belong to the same magnetic field of infinite possibilities, it means that we can have access to all the information and abundance of the Universe. This is how scientists make discoveries, they focus on an intention until they download the information; all of us have the same abilities. We just need discipline. Another fact that is good to know is that some ancient books and scientists suggest that in our DNA we have receptors that connect us with the creative source, which means that we are constantly creating our life. When we understand our relationship with the Universe, we advance in our spiritual journey allowing us to a better life. When we uplift our thoughts and live in a higher state of consciousness, we create a mental state of joy, purpose and the feeling that everything is achievable. We are part of the divine source carrying an infinite power, therefore, always embrace the universal connection where all possibilities exist and be part of the surprising awakening that is happening in our world.

Ergon Emotional Intelligence (EEI)

Then I decided to create the concept of Ergon Emotional Intelligence understanding how our emotions affect our energy vibration, this being the determining factor in our relationship with the Universe. **Ergon** is the root of the word energy in Greek and means work. EEI is the ability to work with your emotions and understand how they affect your energy vibration, this one steadily influences your daily life. EEI is the ability to work with your emotions consciously to create the right energy vibration. It is the knowledge to recognize how any action, habit or behavior provokes a specific energy vibration. Spirituality is linked with our vibrational states, the ones that determine the quality of our lives. EEI goes beyond just managing your emotions; it also includes understanding how they affect your vibrational state. It brings the understanding that any action that you perform is sending a message to the Universe in terms of frequencies. EEI is awareness of your emotional states in terms of energy, and it is also awareness about how crucial it is understanding the behavior of your energy in relation to the Universe.. EEI is basically, understanding our lives in terms of energy. When we understand energy, we become more open-minded and get into field of infinite possibilities, activating our connection with the divine source. As we strengthen the connection with the divine, we get stronger in all aspects of life. Understand our life in terms of energy is fundamental for your spiritual growth. For example, we all know that is good to live in love, but the concept gets more powerful when we understand that love is an emotion with a high frequency which implicate being more powerful and attractive to good things. The same happened with fear, when we understand that is an emotion with a low frequency, implicating vulnerability. EEI wants to emphasis the role of our vibration in our daily lives. Another example of how important is to understand your vibration is when a person is pretending happiness, but their vibration is low and as a result you can observe the person situation that does not match with a high frequency outcome. It matches with low frequencies outcomes. When we consider that we all live in this magnetic field called the Universe where everything is vibrating and reacting based on frequencies, being aware and knowing how to manage our vibrational states should be a priority.

Understanding our lives in terms of energy enhances our abilities to manifest what we really want; it also builds up awareness to realize if what we are doing is convenient or not. For example, when we are in a situation where someone asks you for a donation, if you decide to donate some money, you are sending a message to the Universe that is saying you have more than enough, but if we decide not to donate the message is that you don't have enough. If we analyze these two actions, the first one comes from the feeling of abundance and the other one comes from the feeling of scarcity. The Universe will always respond based on our feelings and emotions. Another example is when analyzing obstinacy. When people are stubborn, they are in a state of rigidness, which is like being constricted and avoiding expansion. In other words, they are not flowing and expanding with the Universe. Remember, we are the Universe, and this one is always expanding, so we should too. Another illustration and very common is when people are upset for the negativity of other people, and they stay talking for long periods of time about the same situation. They don't realize that they are connecting with that negativity and decreasing their frequency. The same happened when we are constantly talking about negative events. Of course, we can talk about negative events, but we must be aware of how much time we spend talking about them and what kind of emotion we are emitting. You need to constantly observe what kind of messages you are sending to the Universe because any action in our physical world has a counterpart in the invisible world. Another case to observe is when you are fighting or arguing with somebody in your mind you are sending a message to the Universe saying that something is wrong, besides if you are one with the Universe, then you are fighting and arguing with yourself as well and decreasing your vibrational state. A common example is when we see religious people criticizing other people that don't follow the doctrine or don't behave properly, they don't realize how hateful they get, nor how unconsciously they are decreasing their frequency. When we become mindful about our energy vibration, we start to balance our lives and get more empowered. We all can recognize many other common behaviors and analyze them in terms of energy to observe how they might be affecting our energy vibration. Our life depends on our vibrational levels, prioritize self-observation, and pursue balance. Being aware of our energetic field is a basic principle.

As I mentioned before emotions determine our life, each emotion is a vibration, and that vibration has a frequency that is sent to the Universe. Considering that frequencies are information, then do you know what kind of information you are sending to the Universe? Always remember the basic principle that love and fear are the two basic emotions ,fear with a low frequency and love with a high frequency. When we notice and observe how the whole system is based in fear ,we should pay more attention and always wonder what kind of emotion predominates in our life. For example, after having an argument with somebody, we can analyze and ask ourselves, what did I said? Was from the side of love or from the side of fear? Or when we are going to make a decision, we can ask, I'm making this decision from the side of love or the side of fear? This practice will help us to get in tone with high frequencies and make us a more loving person with a high vibrational state.

This is about being clear about what kind of behaviors lift your frequencies and the ones that lower them. Frustrations, guilt, regrets, sadness, anger, jealousy, disgust, shame, , disappointment, bitterness, confusion, and despair are low frequency emotions and it is normal to experiment with them but not normal to stick with them. On the other hand, we have the high-frequency emotions like love, gratitude, compassion, kindness, amusement, hope, pride, serenity, confidence, admiration, enthusiasm, astonishment, optimism, joy, happiness, interest, inspiration, satisfaction, excitement, contentment, blissful would be extraordinary for all of us if we manage to live more with these types of positive emotions. Our lives are always oscillating but we are the ones who decide how we want to live our lives, either in a high or low frequency. In simple words, if we want to live in the side of love or in the side of fear, it can be also express as living on the side of the light or on the side of darkness.

When we feel emptiness in our life or feel lack of motivation it means that we need to improve our connection with our higher self or divine source. Dissatisfaction means that we do not have the proper connection with the Universe, which is like resisting its natural flow. Since we are part of the Universe where everything is evolving and expanding, we all have the same lifework, which is advancing in our spiritual journey. One of the main goals in our existence is to learn how to manipulate energy to understand our energy and its behavior in relation to the Universe. The adventure of transformation is a constant improvement of our inner world where outcomes are created. It is looking for balance in any aspect of our life, discerning that balance is perfection. When we enhance our connection with the higher self, we can download any information, but of course, this is achieved when we are focused on an intention without significant issues interfering with our inner peace. It is the same methods the scientists use; they are isolated, concentrated and focused on any specific intention, and then the magic happens when they download information and make significant discoveries. We all can do the same since we all have incredible capacities of creation; we just need to believe in our inner potential, use our time more efficiently and practice the knowledge. It doesn't matter how much knowledge we have. If we don't practice, we will never have the expected results, this is the point where many people fail.(Before talking to me with wisdom, show me your results).The answers we are looking for are present in the universal consciousness. We just need to be conscious and receptive to reap the messages that the Universe is always sending us in different ways.

It is time to get out of so many forced distractions that are interrupting our evolution process. Paying more attention to our emotions is decisive in our daily life. At the end everybody wants and deserves a better life. If we add a subconscious mind plus distractions, it equals an extremely unaware individual, which is a prevalent situation affecting millions of lives. I am pretty sure that every human being wants to be a good person, and everyone understand their behavior as correct, but once again, it is important to be aware that we have been mentally induced to behave against ourselves and these programs resides in your subconscious mind steadily affecting our life. Everybody is receiving the same information over and over, and this information creates the type of people a small group wants. I would recommend not judging people, judging the system, and being more skeptical about everything. When you understand and accept how we all have been living at the mercy of others who obviously don't have the best intentions for humanity, we will have more understanding of other people's negative behaviors, becoming more compassionate and enjoying mental balance.

We need to compromise to live focused and centered, avoiding so many distractions, and always remember that everything begins from within. Work with that unconscious need to seek acceptance, this being a trap with negative consequences. The more focused and authentic we are with ourselves, the more creative and stable we will be. Spend time recognizing and validating our inner power, get rid of those chains that do not belong to our existence and start practicing activities that empower us. Being a good human being requires a lot of self-observation and concentration. Our life is constantly telling us how good or bad we are doing; we just need to observe our life with honesty. Accepting responsibility is another social issue that humanity must solve. We are creators of any outcome, positive or negative, we need to accept any situation, analyze them and make the proper adjustments if is needed. This practice really helps us to reach balance and become better in all aspects. The best antidote to combat this system of corruption is to live in love, not in fear. Learning to love others without judging strengthens us, empowers us and opens doors to the wonders of life. We are all victims, but we don't need to feel like it. We just need to have control of our lives, and being aware of how we have been exposed to twisted information based on fear and separation. Love is the key, is the highest frequency, and the goal is to vibrate as much as possible in a high frequency, which is equivalent to wellbeing.

Practices to raise our frequency.

Our daily life consists of many activities on a regular basis, and these activities are the building blocks of our existence. Engaging in constant healthy practices can bring us the life we expect. Life can be simple and harmonious when we believe more in our inner potential and prioritize the right habits. Get rid of the concept that life must be hard or complicated, being this concept created to make people busy getting busy and away from our divine nature. The main reason for a complicated life is the lack of clarity in our minds. It is just the result of not being committed to the right mental and physical practices. Being engaged in habits that raise our frequency and connect us with the divine power is the path to health, abundance and true love.

Gratitude

My favorite and easiest practice is **gratitude**. When I came to the US with lots of bills and a poor paycheck, I started to practice gratitude. Every time I realized that I was worrying, I switched to gratitude. It took me quite a few years to master it, and I am still working with the skill, but the results are phenomenal, bringing me peace and the ability to manifest the things that I want. The feeling of gratitude is a celebration of our outcomes that benefit our mental and physical health, enhancing our resilience to trauma and raising our levels of optimism. Gratitude is connected to happiness; it erases negativity because joy and despair cannot reside in the same place. Count our blessings and be grateful for our challenges because they are making us stronger and activate our talents and our inner potential. Gratitude is the key to unlocking abundance, happiness, and fulfillment and creates a mindset of positivity. Gratitude changes our focus from scarcity to abundance, from fear to love, from isolation to connection. Gratitude will reshape our thoughts, emotions and actions, renewing our spirit energy vibration.

We need to be grateful in our relationships, recognizing the love, support and company of others, and expressing our gratitude frequently and openly strengthens any relationship. Notice all the abundance that already surrounds us, get immersed in the feeling of gratitude, and create the emotional connection that fuels manifestation. When we are grateful, we are radiating a high-frequency energy that attracts more positive things. Besides, when we send this strong signal to the Universe, this, in turn responds by aligning circumstances and experiences that match our desires.

Sharing what you have is a way of gratitude, from a smile or an act of kindness to more things. Small acts of gratitude will create a positive, potent signal direct to the Universe. Practice generosity by sharing our time, talents, and knowledge send a signal to the Universe saying that we have more than enough. Practicing gratitude will change our lives in many positive ways.

Authenticity

Being true to ourselves, living with high values and analyzing our beliefs will reinforce our integrity. Accepting good quality standards , hold on to our ideals and being moral in all circumstances is the best way to go. Be ourselves before trying to fit in society, stick to our truth, and follow our passions vigorously regardless of the pressure that we are under to act otherwise.

Being authentic means being faithful to who we really are, improving our connection with our inner being, and strengthening our sense of identity. When we are true to ourselves, we will attract more situations or experiences that resonate with us, bringing harmony to ourselves and leading to deeper and more meaningful relationships. Being authentic will increase our frequency of delivering the right outcomes to our lives. Accepting our mistakes and taking responsibility for our actions will enhance our inner power. Always trying to identify the gap between what we are right now and what we want to be brings clarity and direction. Being authentic is to flow to the beat of the Universe, it is to flow just like we are, recognizing our essence and taking advantage of such.

Forgiveness

Forgiveness is a decision and a process that will eventually remove any turmoil from our minds, creating space for healing emotional wounds. Many diseases have negative emotions as their origin, even though the medical industry does not talk about it. In the process of forgiving, we need to understand that every experience we have reflected our inner world. We must accept responsibility for what we experienced and understand that many times, we all act from the subconscious without the intentions of doing any harm. Forgiveness is understanding our nature and others, it is an act of empowerment. When we forgive, we heal and improve our connection with others and the Universe. The act of absolution should be for us and others, when we let it go, we are releasing our spirit and embracing inner peace. Guiltiness is an earthy conceptis not valid in the Universe. When we analyze the principle of attraction or the principle of cause and effect, we can understand that whatever happened to us was a self-created outcome. We must take responsibility for any event that comes into our life without the feeling of guilt, blame or rejection.

Surround with the right people.

The people we choose to surround ourselves with will eventually shape the way we think, behave and even how we dress. They will affect the way we perceive and manage life. We always should surround ourselves with people who are going to lift us higher and look out for our best interest. We need to look for honest people who share our core values, support ourselves and challenge us to improve our lives. We want to spend time with people who believe in expansion and have a growth mindset. Keep in mind that attracting this kind of person requires that internally we are craving for improvement.

Make a connection with nature.

Research studies show that people who spend more time connected with nature are usually happier and healthier by reducing cortisol levels, balancing blood pressure, and decreasing levels of anxiety and depression. Connect with nature and feel gratitude while contemplating its beauty. Nature is beauty is pure, sacred energy of the Universe flowing just like it is, without the interference of human programming. Nature is us in another expression, and it always looks for balance. Walk barefoot and absorb the healing energy that emanates from the earth(grounding). Look for quiet places to contemplate, this infuses ourselves with serenity. Embracing the essence of the Universe by spending more time in nature increases our neural activity, improving our mindfulness skills, which is crucial to our self-improvement.

Exercise

Our bodies are designed to move and everything in our body is moving. Not moving creates stiffness, which is the opposite to ease or relaxation. Exercise triggers the production of endorphins, which help to relieve pain and boost your mood and energy. Exercise positively affects any organ of your body, especially the heart, which is the manifestation organ, the most magnetic organ in our body. It does not matter how old we are. We need to move every day and practice strength exercises that work as an anti-aging agent. Exercise restores the natural flow of energy in your body. If we remember the story of the Sumerians, we were made to be slaves. Our bodies are made to move.

Meditation

Meditation is probably one of the best practices to quiet our minds and have a better connection with our spiritual realm. The habit of meditation brings inner peace, helps us to be mindful and will also assist us to get rid of unnecessary attachments. People who practice meditation become more inspired and enthusiastic about life. They are committed to self-improvement and have a better attitude to face life challenges. It is a mental exercise where we engage in concentration, contemplation or reflection. It is a step to acquire mental discipline. When we meditate, we develop awareness, boost clarity and elevate our spirit. There are different types of meditation ,could be guided by someone, and could be transcendental, where we repeat a mantra. Even sitting and contemplate nature is a form of meditation. Some researchers shows that meditation can change the brain structure, increasing gray matter density in the hippocampus, which means a higher concentration of nerve cell bodies in that region, which is crucial for memory and learning, also suggesting potentially improved cognitive function. Meditation can prompt the brain to shift from those high-alert waves to the slower, more relaxed waves that are linked to states of calm, deep focus and sleep. Meditation should be a daily practice that will promote emotional health, reduce high blood pressure and slow cellular aging. Meditating twenty minutes a day can make a great positive difference in many aspects of our lives.

Final Thoughts

At this point,, you have all the necessary ingredients to make a flavorful recipe that you can enjoy for the rest of your life. How committed can you be to yourself? When you know and understand that you are connected to the field of infinite possibilities. Within each of you, there is a divine and eternal nature that distinguishes you as an exceptionally powerful entity. Probably the main reasons most people don't accomplish greatness during their lives is because of their lack of commitment, bad decisions, poor habits, limiting beliefs and lack of mental discipline. You can connect with your higher self to find your purpose on this planet and live a meaningful life with joy and fulfilment. Validate what you really are, acknowledge your mental power and feed your mind with good thoughts and emotions to align yourself with the divine source. This is the moment when you can find your life purpose, the opportunity to live your life wholly and in a constant energized state.

Believe in yourself and don't look for external validation, which is a trap. Be true to yourself and embrace who you are, don't live up to society's expectations because, most of the time, they are not align with your inner truth. Society's rules and expectations restrain your true potential and lower your frequencies. Don't be afraid to think differently,I personally experienced rejection from friends and family for not behaving as they expect, but in the end, it has been worth it. I resisted the society's pressure, and I used it as a motivation to believe more in myself. I dedicated extra time to work on myself improvement, keeping always in mind the phrase that spark my transformation process:"My exterior world is a manifestation of my inner world." Your daily mental processes are invariably creating your life. I started to avoid internal conflicts between who I am and who I was trying to be. I started to acknowledge my divine nature, I experienced physical loneliness, but I knew I was not alone since I'm connected to the rest of the Universe. You need to flow just like you are. Otherwise, you will be flowing against the natural stream of the Universe.

This one is always perceiving your vibration, and you cannot fake happiness when you feel sad because the Universe is always perceiving your frequencies. You can lie to yourself but not to the Universe. Accept yourself and your experiences you cannot fail at being yourself.

Acceptance is a state of mind that allows you to embrace whatever is happening in your life without resistance or judgment, and thus, you will avoid suffering. When you accept your present moment, you validate your emotional experience, giving space to learn, change and grow. You are expanding with the Universe. This one wants you to keep expanding and evolving. Make the commitment to keep your mind open to learn new things and accept changes. Self-transformation is an ongoing process. Elevate your understanding to continually refine your worldview and be more assertive in your decisions and beliefs. Keep exploring the extensive territories of your mind with curiosity and determination; this will drive you to transcend challenges and improve your existence. The Universe always wants you to be fine and bring the knowledge to keep improving your life. But sometimes, you are so immersed in absurd beliefs that you are not receptive to listening to the messages that come to you to improve your actual status When you stay in the familiar zone and prefer to follow most people, either for that need of acceptance or lack of courage, you will stay in the same situation forever, which means stagnation. When I try to analyze this behavior that keeps people in suffering, I understand the presence of various factors that interferes in people's transformation process; besides that need to belong to the herd, they have a high level of Fixable Unconscious Reception Impairment(FURI) and people love to highlightfears originating from all those limiting and destructive beliefs established by a few. But there is always a way out, you just need determination. A good way to start creating new mental habits and strengthen your willpower is by breaking it down into smaller steps. Start doing little things that might feel uncomfortable at the beginning. For example, exercise fifteen minutes a day, decrease the time you spend watching tv, go to bed half an hour earlier, stop eating so much junk food, and engage in activities that eventually will bring wellbeing. When you start doing things differently step by step, your brain starts creating new neural pathways that eventually will become a habit. Incorporate new practices in your daily life, for example I recommend Feng Shui.

Feng Shui an assessable practice for everyone and a great ally for your journey through life. Feng Shui originated in the Chinese culture evidently less contaminated from the Occidental culture, and with more information about energy behavior, Feng Shui is the art of arranging spaces to achieve harmony and balance. The purpose is to get your environment in alignment with who you are and where you want to go. Your surroundings are the energy in which you have an intimate relationship. To work with your spaces is fundamental, your home, office or wherever you spend most of the time. Each cardinal point of your living space affects different aspects of your life. For example, the north area of any room is related to professional opportunities ,the element associated with it is water, and the color is blue. Knowing this, that area should always be clean and organized with some details in blue color and a water fountain or something that relates to water. Southeast is related to love; the element is earth, and the color is yellow. Looking for a relationship? Use some details with yellow color, place a terracotta pot as the earth element, and display a painting of a couple, for example, or pairs of your election. This practice regulates the energy flow and boosts your desires. In general, all areas of your living space should be clean and organized. Observe where you have trash cans. Your fridge should be organized and without old food, avoid cluttering, which in terms of energy is stagnation. Don't allow empty bottles that are trash. Constantly move objects to different spaces at least once a month with the new or full moon. Energy needs to flow in all aspects of your life, run your life holistically, always paying attention to your surroundings as well as your feelings, thoughts, and emotions.

This practice will boost your connection with your higher self. I have been practicing Feng Shui for three years, and my experience has been great and fruitful. The only way to enjoy the wonders of Feng Shui is by practicing it. Other practices should be aromatherapy, which influences your senses and regulates your emotional states, and listens to healing sounds. These ones improve your vibration by the effect of resonance. All these practices will also regulate your brain waves. My best advice is that you should be interested in topics and activities that up lift your life and bring well-being, evaluate your distractions, and establish priorities, because everything is there waiting for you to make the decision. Making decisions is changing, evolving, is loving yourself. Incorporate these new practices in your life, and create new neural networks. Your brain loves it, rewarding you with good mental health. Remember, the Universe is mental where any process of creation starts; and most people are creating the reality that they don't want because of their high levels of FURI (fixable unconscious reception impairment).

I must emphasize how important it is to be consciously receptive and how detrimental it is to be unconsciously stubborn and keep the same routine. I personally have seen so many people living in constant pain and despair, accepting as normal their situation. The common factor among these people is that they all have lost their capacity to accept new ways to see life. It is crucial to make changes and, be receptive to new ideas and concepts, always listen with the desire of knowing the truth and understanding, so you don't miss out on accurate information that potentially can improve your life. Take time for self-observation, it is the skill that will build up your validation. This requires courage and humility to change your limiting beliefs. Probably the best way to avoid this common problem is to commit yourself to keep your curiosity active, always asking and investigating. You validate yourself when you are always listening, and your priority is understanding. Remove that need to be right, it is like a mental disease interfering with your spiritual progress Suffering is one of the results of this harmful habit, Some people say that suffering is part of life, but it doesn't have to be for long periods of time. Self-validation is not in other people's hands. When you believe in yourself, you are validating what you really are, you are reconnecting with your higher self that always has been there to guide you throughout life, and this capacity was lost due to all those dogmas induced by fear. Stubbornness and fear go against your true nature of being expanding and evolving steadily, it causes energetic rigidity that's inhibits proper body functioning, creating pain. Being receptive is crucial to having a better understanding of life and, therefore ,living a healthy one. Always observe around you, pay attention to behavioral patterns in others and analyze their results. This will bring you an idea of the dos and don'ts of life. We all have great potential if we accept it, believe in it and practice it. It is extremely important to develop your own criteria, not the criteria that others want you to have and this is also self-validation, the state of being where you recognize your over-flowing potential, is a state where lack does not exist.

Abundance is everywhere, and you are abundant by nature. As soon as the egg and the sperm make a synergetic connection called fertilization, you have all the necessary resources to develop as a human, and you still possess all kinds of resources to keep moving up throughout life. It is important to keep this concept in mind as much as possible, and it will help you reprogramming your subconscious mind, from a state of vulnerability to a state of security, trust, and empowerment. Remember you have anything you need. It is about trust, faith and understanding the principles that rule the Universe.

It took me some time to start validating myself, growing up in a catholic family and studying in a catholic private school, I was influenced by many limiting beliefs; I was always looking for validation. But my curiosity saved my life, and help me to find the knowledge that brought me hope, determination and self-approbation. It has been a long road but so far, my life is getting better as time goes by. Understanding energy and its behavior in relation to the Universe is the key to creating anything you want. Validate your role in the Universe and believe that this will always respond to your vibration, sending you the necessary messages to direct your life on the right path, you just need to be receptive. Evaluate your receptivity, and acknowledge the harmful behavior of being stubborn that, most of the time, is a consequence of living unconsciously, naively and feeding your ego excessively. Having a reactive life is totally injurious. It means disconnection from your higher self and impedes the life you expect. Your life needs to be created consciously, and self-awareness is your top priority so you can work with your second priority, which is reprogramming your subconscious mind consciously. The subconscious mind is very convenient, giving us the ability to react without thinking or analyzing, but at the same time, it can be harmful if you don't start changing all those imprinted programs that interfere with your personal progress. You can take many courses or seminars, which is a good thing, but your focus must be on reprogramming those destructive beliefs that reside in your subconscious and are constantly holding you back. Develop a growth mindset and work with your expansion. This can be achieved observing your internal conversation. What you say about you and your life is constantly programming yourself and designing your life. Develop your mental discipline by trying to become conscious, trying to understand your emotional states and their origin. Keep in mind how emotions are connected to the subconscious mind which has been exposed to many programs since you were born.

When you are born, your true nature is intact. As you grow up and start receiving external information, your true nature starts to decline as well as your inner power. As you grow, your ego starts to develop, and this one is a tendency towards self-affirmation. It directs your behavior. It is the psychic instance through which you recognize yourself. The ego makes you live hypnotize and live your life distant from your essence. The need for control and always being right is generated from the ego, although a balanced ego can give a person confidence in their abilities and decision-making skills You must pay attention because, many times, what is good for the ego is not good for your true nature. It is crucial to observe what kind of behaviors come from the egoic mind. Can you understand how important it is to live in a state of awareness? It is your responsibility to recover your universal talents, the ones that are activated through the power of self-love, empathy, and compassion. Self-love starts with self-validation and getting rid of all negative emotions like fears, frustrations, and regrets. Living in love is living in a vibrant state of mind where many things are possible. You must question where your life is going and analyze your ideas, beliefs, and actions to see if they align with your desires.

If you don't practice, you forget.

You must make constant adjustments in your life, especially about certain religious concepts. Understanding the fractality of the Universe, where we all belong and where every part has its own role and is responsible for its performance, it is obvious to conclude that there is no room for a single entity to have control of everything. My personal theory is about multiple entities assisting us during life, there are positive entities and negative entities or high-frequency entities and low-frequency entities. We are all part of the same whole, and everyone oversees their own evolution. Being part of a whole means that your nature brings the desire to cooperate with each other. Observe how good it feels when you help others. In the Christian mythology, they have the angels, entities that want to assist us in this journey, but I'm convinced that these entities can be of any kind and not necessarily have to be easy to the eye. They can have different shapes and levels of evolution. Some people say that we have had the same guardian angel since we were born, but I think they are different ones throughout life. If the law of attraction says "like attracts like," we will probably have spiritual guides according to our vibration; therefore, if we are in a low vibration, we won't receive the protection and guidance that you expect. When you are in a high vibration you can observe many synchronicities in your favor rather than when you are in a low vibration, bringing lots of setbacks.

Numerology is one of the ways the spiritual realm communicates with us. When you pay attention to numbers that shows up repeatedly and look for the meaning, you are discovering the messages and demonstrating interest.Furthermore your angels will communicate more often through numbers and synchronicities. You can establish good communication with the positive Universal Realm and receive their guidance., they are also receptive to your vibration. I recommend the practice of meditation. When you meditate, you get disconnected from those external inputs that provoke distortion in your vibrational states, regulating your vibration and enhancing a better connection with the divine source. Life can be enjoyable in most cases; the key is your vibration.

We need to be mindful of those elements that cut out your high frequencies, especially those negative emotions caused by emotional wounds from the past that are stagnant in your subconscious mind. When people don't heal their wounds, they spend their life hurting others and living in a low frequency. If we apply the Law of Oneness where we are all connected, while we are hurting others, we are hurting ourselves and as a result we are constantly experiencing negative outcomes, like health issues. There are many causes for health issues, but I dare to say that bad emotions are on top of the list. You need to observe how many emotions are trigger from your beliefs, perceptions and the people around you. Choose wisely the people you spend more time with.

Relationships can bring many emotional disturbances, and they come with conflicts at all levels. Most of them are due to the need for control. This one is related to your ego and imprinted programs in your subconscious. Most people have a desire for a LTR, but most people are not ready to have a harmonious one. Why haven't we been educated to have happy and fruitful relationships? **Analyze, please.** Relationships also start from within. How is the relationship with yourself? Before having an LTR you need to heal emotional wounds from the past, love yourself, and eliminate the need for control. You will always attract people who are aligned with your vibration. Remember, your external world reflects your internal emotional states. You must transform yourself into the person that you want as a partner. Relationships are a mirror of yourself, bringing you the opportunity of self-observation. Of course this requires humility and self-honesty. Relationships can be a gift for your personal growth if both individuals decide to advance together. It is a connection between two fragments of energy provoking synergy if they are well aligned. In simple words, synergy is when one plus one is more than two. A harmonious relationship can be immensely powerful and creative in terms of energy. Sharing your body and soul with someone is a privilege. Having sex is a fusion betwixt strong vibrations emanated from each person involved, and these emanations are messages sent to the Universe and can be powerful if the act of sex originates from true love. When you share the same intentions with your partner, these are magnified. It is good to know every time you experience intercourse, you are exchanging ethereal fluids with the other person, affecting your spiritual progress, either positively or negative. You need to evaluate what kind of person you bring to your life, always considering if that person adjusts to your values and has the desire to understand your points of view. Considering that we tend to imitate the habits of those with whom we interact the most, furthermore choosing a life partner is a complex and crucial decision that will affect your whole existence. Having an LTR is like having an ally to assist in your life transformation. It is the experience where you can demonstrate true love, becoming more flexible and tolerant between many other things. If you really want a healthy LTR, start working with your inner self, In the end, the better you become, the better you are going to be your significant one. You need to keep in mind how your past can affect your present moment. It is important to recall memories to heal emotional wounds, many of which occurred during your childhood, giving you the opportunity to enter your relationship emotionally healthy.

Most of your parents did not have the knowledge to raise children, they all try to do their best, but they just followed what they learned from their parents when information was not as accessible as today. Parenting these days can be difficult due to many distractions. I can observe some weakness in many parents due to a lack of knowledge to deal with the evolution of their children. There is an urgency for actual parents to educate themselves and reevaluate their methods of education if they want to have satisfactory results. Stability in the household is the basic desire, and this can be materialize if parents start to put more attention on their inner work. It is important to be aware of what kind of emotions predominate in the house, there is a term called **limbic resonance** which means that emotions can be shared with those whom we have close connection. For example, if the parents are living in a constant emotional stress their children can absorb those negative vibrations through their limbic system. When we consider that the limbic system is the most developed part of the brain during childhood, we can expect that negative emotions around them will affect their emotional and physical health. I have been observing this situation for years where couples with toxic relationships have children with asthma and even cancer. I encourage anyone to recognize how important is to be constantly aware of their emotional states and to understand life in terms of energy so everyone can enjoy the amazing wonders of the Universe. Any type of relationship requires a profound self-knowledge, clear intentions, and authentic sense of love. Most of the time fear is the predominant emotion in relationships, you can shift to the emotion of love as you avoid those feelings of having control of everything and the compulsion to be always right. The Universe is flexible, and you need to respect the free will that applies for all of us. Before getting into any type of relationship or having children make necessary internal adjustments to experience the results you deserve. Life is not a random game; life is like an equation in which several factors must be taken into consideration to have a desired outcomes. You need clarity to define what you really want, clarity about yourself perception, accepting and understanding your strengths and weaknesses. Another factor is commitment where you are consistent with your behavior, and ensure you do what you say you are going to do. The third factor is courage to trust your inner self and do not spill in the pitfall of pleasing society. A good life requires control in all aspects, especially your mental control and discipline.

Self-control is part of your mental discipline. You can only have control over your emotional states and mental processes. The need to have control over external things most of the time is a reactive behavior based in your unconscious patterns. Avoiding having control over others frees us from the frustration of wanting others to conform to our expectations. Do not spend so much energy with the external world, find your way back to your inner being and discover your innate power that is waiting for you to be activated. Pay attention to what kind of virtues you need to develop, leading by example is how you have influence in others. Focusing on your inner work not only leads to serenity, but it also lights the way for others. Is fundamental to master mindfulness and self-awareness, these are the best tools to develop self-observation. You need to know what is going on in your subtle realm. Everything starts from within, validating and loving yourself is an effective way to achieve a higher spiritual state. I want you to stop and analyze, why we have never been taught to love ourselves? One of the answers is, because love is a high frequency, the level of frequency that make us powerful. If you want to recover your power love yourself, love others, love everything, because everything is part of the Oneness.

I started to learn to love myself after my 50 years.when my last relationship ended fifteen years ago, during that relationship I discovered the Law of Attraction, when I learned the role of vibrations in my life, it was the moment when I started to validate myself and paying more attention to my emotional states. As soon as you get mindful, you start loving yourself. It took me a year to quit my relationship where many times I was in a low vibration. When I started to understand and assimilate the Law of Attraction, I was trying to observe my thoughts and think positively, but my anguish was creating a low vibration, it was the moment where I realized how important and urgent it was to get out of the relationship even though I was very much in love. I was learning that is not what you pretend to look like, is your vibration what really creates your life. As soon as I assimilated the law of attraction concept, my relationship was over. Then I came to the United States six months after the breakup where I dedicated my life to get educated in many aspects of life understanding how important is to have a broad spectrum of information if you want to make good decisions throughout your life. In my case changing my mindset took me quite a few years and eventually I achieved a significant change in my life.

Changes can be triggered from the need of improvement, especially when you want to have a better life. You can start to question why people must go through so many negative outcomes? When ask to yourself about the cause of so much misfortune? You can understand that ignorance is the main cause, but keeping yourself ignorant is a choice especially these days when information is accessible to everyone. I must emphasize how being naive and distracted can be so harmful to any human. Prioritizing the search for knowledge, practicing self-awareness and acknowledging the essence of your true self are key points to design the life that you want. Since I was young, I developed the ability to observe people to find out what really works to improve my life and what doesn't. Observing people's attitudes, behaviors and beliefs and their results can give us enough information to figure out what is good for us and what is not. At my 66 years I have collected a vast amount of information to conclude that humanity has been exposed to misconstrued information. My biggest concern is to see the people around me going through situations that can be avoided when you have the courage to stop accepting many things that we have been told. Believing and understanding our nature is fundamental for our well-being. We all have desires and want to achieve goals thus we need to prepare ourselves first, working consistently with our emotions and perceptions and reprogramming our subconscious mind. Educate yourself as much as possible in all aspects of life and everything will be accommodated according to your desires. Spend your energy on activities that empower you and keep the balance between distractions and self-improvement. Get ready for the things that you want they are just waiting for you.

When I opened the restaurant in 1988, during the opening act, at one point I said, "I want to feed the world, including bodies and souls."That just came to my mind because, at that moment, I was discovering metaphysics, so I was in a spiritual mode. Eventually, I realized that feeding souls means bringing the knowledge to understand our true nature, our spirit and our life .Humanity needs to get involved in an uplifting knowledge of hope, empowerment and encouragement. After I closed the restaurant in 2009, I decided to dedicate my spare time to educating myself to be prepared for eventually feeding the souls, bringing spiritual knowledge to whoever is receptive. Now I comprehend that in these moments where the future of humanity is uncertain, we all need to be prepared fot the unknown, . This is the precise moment to make important decisions toward a better future for us and humanity where we are the critical mass to change the global situation, each one of us can change the world with autocracy.

It is time to make a turn and take a new path of understanding, where you learn to see things from a higher spiritual perspective. Where you have more than enough power to change your reality and your surroundings. Your imagination is the foundation of faith and hope, you can imagine, dream, and have the desire to advance toward a brighter future.

It is in the active search for our virtues that we find our purpose and happiness. A person of virtue makes the progression from knowing what is right to do and what is not right. It is living a human life in accordance with reason, courage, purpose, and devotion. Virtues are attitudes that enable humans to live in a proper way, with honesty, compassion, integrity, and respect. These should be present in your daily life being these active elements to exalt your existence. Paying attention to what kind of virtues you must develop brings you to a higher level of consciousness. The goal is to be aware of your behaviors, thoughts, and emotions, which might sound easy but require a lot of practice. To have a good life does not require so much physical effort. It requires mental discipline to develop the ability of self-observation to be conscious of your flaws, thus create habits that align with your desires. Remember, you are the prey of your subconscious mind if you are not conscious. Self-awareness and mindfulness should be priorities on anyone life, I must emphasize this because unconsciousness is a destructive habit spread all over the planet. Being present and aware of your behavior and emotions magnifies your inner power. A significant positive change will come when you change your behavior, thoughts, feelings and emotions, and the only way to do it is to be aware of how you really are. I can see so much unconsciousness among all kinds of people, not matter the level of education. You can observe many people professionally successful, but their personal lives is unfortunate due to the lack of balance, the most important job is working with yourself and your mental discipline. When you do your inner work, the Universe recognizes that you are ready and will respond to your desires. Many people don't achieve their dreams because they never get to know themselves. Knowing yourself and knowing what's going on on the planet are your responsibility.

Do you know what are the agendas of some institutions of the planet, like 2030 agenda of the United Nations? In simple words, it is an agenda of slavery, it consists of seventeen points that superficially sounds fantastic but when you understand the background of these seventeen point it is scary. Take your time and investigate this agenda and realize how important is to work with your inner being, which is the solution to any situation in your present life, remember your internal world reflects your outer world. Reevaluate what kind of things you are spending your energy on, if they are bringing wellbeing, or if they are keeping you in the same situation. Our planet is facing drastic changes; some people are awakening, and some others will stay thinking and acting the same way. These are the ones that probably have the hardest time. Evolving is our nature, and not changing is stagnation. It is like going against the entire Universe. As you evolve and enhance your spiritual connection with the divine, you raise your frequency, and the frequency of our planet will also rise, which means that negativity on the planet will dissipate.

Most people agree that spirituality is fundamental in anyone's life but working with your spirituality require constant self-observation to be able to make the appropriate adjustments in your thoughts, emotions, and behaviors. It is highly recommended to observe how you spend your powerful energy, pay attention if your behavior has its origin in the ego and the need for control or is a behavior that comes from love and confidence. Any behavior will carry a frequency, you decide if you want to live in a low or a high vibrational state. Our planet is facing a battle between light and darkness, can you recognize your role in this battle? Getting out and protesting about the things that we don't want is the common practice and sometimes it might work, but what really can trigger a significant change in the planet is raising the frequency of the whole planet. As humanity starts opening their minds and rejecting all those destructive beliefs and distractions that are constantly decreasing our vibrations, all evil will start to lose control. And this is happening right now, we all together need to be advocates in this Probably the first step is to accept responsibility for any outcome, either good or bad. Any situations that come to your life have been created by yourselves, sometimes conscious, some other times unconscious, but we are the ones who created them. If you develop the habit of analyzing why you are experiencing a negative outcome and try to figure out why it is happening, eventually ,you can learn what kind of things you are doing that provoke those unwanted results. In other words you will start tuning your lives to a more meaningful one. I can hear all the time people emphasizing that we are not perfect, which is another limiting belief, because perfection is balance, I want to say it again if everything is good or positive there is no balance. In any mistake that we make, there is the opportunity to learn and to make ourselves stronger. Balance predominates everywhere, we don't need to carry with thoughts or feeling of imperfection or guiltiness these are terms created to disempower humanity.

It is time to understand energy, understand the Universal principles and know how to apply them to your life, is the moment to learn how to be conscious and be able to decipher this crossroad established by a small group of people. Stop supporting concepts that do not lead us to satisfactory outcomes. It is time to accept, acknowledge and believe in our inner power. This is an ongoing process where we must pass many levels. The scale is infinite; therefore, we should motivate ourselves to overcome each level and be able to enjoy all the opportunities that life offers us. There is a common life level where frustrations and worries predominate; this is the level that supports scarcity. What level of life do you want to reach? It is your decision to either stay in your status quo or start working with your inner being and move up. Be aware of your feelings to understand if they are triggered by a mindset of lack or abundance. Be aware that the Universe strives to manifest your beliefs, limitations, and judgments as reality. Being conscious is key, the skill that will uncover the real you. Practicing self-awareness as much as you can will make you a better person. When you observe some people's negative behaviors, don't judge them. Most of the time, they are not aware of their behavior. Instead, they think about the possibilities of being just like them. Remember, we all have been exposed to induced perception; to be, believe and behave like the powerful ones want .Analyze yourself and try to answer questions like what kind of movements you support, how you spend your time, what kind of activities you are engage in, and how productive and balanced you have been lately?

We all need to get out of collective hypnosis, and this hypnosis is the result of many programs running in our subconscious mind affecting our behavioral and emotional responses. It is time to be less emotional and more reasonable, always trying to understand based on facts, not based on what you just have been told. Take your time and always observe your surroundings with your analytical mind. There is no need for so much scarcity, pain, stress, suffering and diseases. All these unwanted outcomes have their origin in the programs we are carrying out daily. Everything is a design that has been in constant progress for thousands of years. The knowledge that empowers human beings has been on the planet since the beginning of time but was transmitted to humanity backward, and humanity is always creating the reality that they want. It is important to observe if the official version matches what we are experiencing. Can you analyze if the situation on the planet is getting better or if there is more chaos every day? Have you wondered why? If the mass media is promoting anew normality, it is time to question everything. If mass media is promoting a leader that looks perfect and has proper talking probably, it is the worst one, and when they put all the energy demonizing some leaders, it is because that person goes against their dark agenda, the agenda that includes wars, segregation, human trafficking, transhumanism, lack of freedom etc.

Most people don't have an idea of the magnitude of lies to which we have been subjected. Accepting and supporting the official version generally results in calamity. All the responsibility is on each one of, and you must investigate, inquire, and have your own criteria, not the criteria that a few people want you to have. Prioritize investigation, nobody is so busy, is just about priorities. Looking for the knowledge that creates well-being should be at the top of your priority list. Remember, many of your priorities have been established by people that don't really care about you. It is urgent to start reprograming your subconscious mind from where your life manifests. Make decisions and act because action is the activity that will make yourself more secure, don't expect to feel secure if you don't act. When you act, you are practicing, and as you practice, you get more self-confident. Always look for new experiences as they mean expansion, a good spirit is in constant expansion.

We are highly intelligent people with many ideas, and together, we can make a better world. The power it is in your hands, and it will always be if you awake and start creating your life consciously. You can change this collective hypnosis with awareness and courage, trusting in your inner power to change this reality that is harming humanity. It is sad for me to see people with the best intentions of being a good human being and enjoying a meaningful life, but their results are not what they want. This happens when you are living your life so naively, which is the cause of many problems in human society. This is a problem that affects all of us, and we need to accept it. Being unaware is not responsible and brings lots of unnecessary complications. Many times, when you are naive, you are supporting things that go against your inner being. Life can be easier when you have the right practices and control of your mental processes, and most important you need to be aware of how your mind has been affected by external programs that do not favor you.

This is a benevolent Universe where unity and cooperation are natural laws. Furthermore, the Universe is waiting for you to take the first step in your transformation process. You all can move from where you are to where you want to be, this is achievable if you act, reprograming your subconscious mind and raising your frequency. Keep in mind as much as possible how you have been exposed to mental programs that create energy imbalance and obstruction in your energy flow, which can result in all types of physical and mental conditions Each one of you is responsible for your energetic balance, which leads to a better self. You are a human mosaic, and each one of you has an important role in this existence. You came to this world to understand and learn how to manage your energy. Nobody can change their life until they change their energy vibration that is constantly affecting your true nature. The one you need to enhance practicing the divine states of loving, kindness, compassion, empathic, joy, and equanimity. Changing is evolving. It is expanding your mind to allow your thought process to grow. It permits you to see things from another perspective, bringing a greater understanding of life and leading you to progress, which is the most important aspect of this journey. When you evolve, you leave your old ways and become a better person. Evolving makes you more compassionate, empathic, and magnetic to attract good things. It is worth it to prioritize time to shift your energy and create the things that you always wanted. Don't waste your life, set your goals high, stop thinking about the things that don't work for you, start thinking about what can be good for you and ask to the Universe how to achieve it. Improve your communication with the Universe and the celestial beings. Eventually, you will feel more confident, and your life will be based on more love and less fears. If you want to live a life that is bigger than anybody that you currently have in your family, it is unreasonable for you to expect them to understand what you are going to do. You just need to believe in yourself and your ideas. Solitude is the price you must pay when you start to grow; it is better to be hated for what you are than to be loved for what you are not. Begin with a promise to yourself to be truthful, honest and factual about who you are and your relationship to yourself, other people, and the rest of the Universe. This is what is going to bring yourself to the level that you deserve.

We live in an unbalanced system, sustained by our ignorance, it is time to develop a critical mind to analyze by yourself and have your own conclusions. It is time to make decisions that propel your life to a state of plenitude. This is the moment of self-validation, self-knowledge, and self-observation. Yes, everything starts with us. Distractions are assassinating humanity. Prioritize your time, your habits, and your curiosity. Avoid all those rigid patterns of thinking and always open your mind to possibilities. The planet Earth could be flat, and the moon might be an artificial satellite; these are possibilities that you can understand if you investigate. When you do your own research, you find clues that support the global scam to which we have been exposed, be more inquisitive about everything you have been told. Living in a mental comfort zone is not the best option to improve your life. Mental comfort is a habit that keeps people in a state of ignorance, supporting concepts that can be detrimental to their existence. We have been programmed in a very subtle way, where we are not aware of the process. It is required to develop the habit of being aware and inquisitive. Do not accept things without investigating their origin. Many events in this world have a distraction as objective, deviating people from their inner work and lessening their frequency. The new normality should be, to have more conversations about the internal work that we all must accomplish and how to do it When we share with people where we are highly connected having conversations about new ideas, self-improvement will open channels to new possibilities. If just by ourselves we put an intention in the Universe, it goes with lots of power, but if two people or more are connected with the same intention, the signal to the Universe is going to be high-powered. Observe your daily conversations and how trivial they can be, and maybe, you can start to get used to more meaningful conversations. Surround yourself with people with whom you can talk about deep topics, people who are curious and eager for innovation. Meditate, write in a journal, ask questions, spend more time alone and expand your curiosity. Keep in mind that everything starts from within. As you work with your inner being, you start to become a better human being. As you love yourself, you are more genuine in loving others, accepting yourself brings a profound acceptance of others, being kind to yourself leads to quality of kindness to others. When you work with yourself, you increase your capabilities to achieve what you want, avoiding frustrations that many people carry for the rest of their lives. There are many types of frustration but what is important to highlight is that frustrated people unconsciously are always throwing out their emotional garbage to others. Being a good person requires intense inner work based on mindfulness, mental discipline, consistency and spiritual self-esteem.

We are part of a quantum field where everything is connected. Your thoughts and emotions are steadily influencing this energetic field. Learning how to consciously activate this quantum field and create the life that you want is probably your main goal in this life. When you live in harmony, your energetic field is strong, reflecting health and liveliness. On the other hand, emotional imbalance creates all types of negative outcomes like toxic relationships and illnesses. To learn how to operate this quantum field is an easy task, what is hard is to convince people to acquire consistency in their daily practices. It requires time and effort to harmonize your thoughts, emotions, and intentions with your expectations, and these must vibrate at the same frequency. What is your level of positive thoughts during the day? Are you paying attention to your daily thoughts? What is the origin of your intentions? Are they come from the emotion of love or fear? How high are your expectations? Does your personal life resonate with your expectations? Usually, your expectations carry a high frequency, then you must work with your energetic field to resonate energetically with your expectations. How disciplined are you? What kind of activities are you engaged in during the day? Your daily routine is the foundation of success and wellbeing, and you need to pay more attention to your physical and mental habits. How do you spend your time? Time is the most appreciated asset. But we have been induced to be distracted as much as possible. The origin of the word distraction in Latin is distrahere, dis meaning apart, and trahere meaning drag, distraction is out of action or dragged away from the task. Distraction is the opposite of success. That's why they are always trying to keep us distracted. Poverty, diseases, and vulnerable people are some of the goals for humanity. Understanding what is really happening on the planet is the way out of so much decay. Being aware that you have been lied all your life is essential to stimulate and compromise yourself to change your way of thinking. You can be wrong in many aspects of your life; you need to accept that you have been living in a falsehood since our second civilization, accepting lies, wars and strange spiritual practices that keep people distracted and away from their full potential. The power is within you, and you just need the courage and humility to accept that you have been mentally affected by induced programs that can be detrimental to your existence. If you want to understand and know the truth, it is fundamental to spend more time educating yourself on many topics available to understand and improve your life.

I can experience all the time how people repeat things without any investigation, and they just do it because most people say it. For example, there are people who still think that eggs raise your cholesterol, or cooking with seed oils is better for your health, or say that diabetes is a genetic disease. Many times, what people inherit are the same mental and physical behaviors that lead to the same health issues. For example, in my family, my grandfather was diabetic ,eventually my mother was also diabetic, and doctors always tell me that I was going to be diabetic. Be aware of any asseveration that comes to your live before accepting it as a fact, especially from the medical industry. Health is a big issue on our planet and is not well handled. The most beautiful asset at the third age is to be healthy, mentally and physically. It is a privilege that you earn throughout life. Understanding how to manage energy is key to attracting abundance, and health. Don't sacrifice your health working so hard. Work with yourself as much as you can. Eventually you will believe more in yourself and feel more empowered, avoiding the need of accepting false diagnoses. When I turn fifty, I woke up with pain in my shoulders. I went to the doctor and he told me "After fifty years old, everybody has arthritis." It is obvious that I did not accept. But if I had accepted it, I would have arthritis today. Because the normal practice is that as soon as you get out of the doctor's office, you tell everybody you know that you have been diagnosed with arthritis. In general cases if you accept the diagnose and talk about the illness constantly plus your thoughts about it, means that you are programing your subconscious mind and eventually will be real. I rather would be cautious with diagnoses. Most health issues are due to mental or physical habits, and we just need mental discipline to change any harmful pattern that I creating your illness. The best example is people with diabetes, the first mistake they make is to accept that is a genetic condition, the second mistake is to take insulin and keep eating whatever they want. What we inherited are the bad habits, that ones we need to get rid of I repeat quite a few times daily "I'm strong and healthy" besides doing the right practices of course. <u>One of the main indicators of your inner being is your health.</u> Tell me how is your health, and I'm going to tell you how are your thoughts, emotions and feelings.

We need to be more analytical about anything we say, and there are always factors to be analyzed and things that we can do to fix any health situation. This applies to everything, it is important to develop a growth mindset where you can have a broad idea of everything. This is what being open-minded means. It is important to become more analytic before accepting any concept, especially when it is about our health. If our whole body regenerates in ten years on average, it means that we can recover from most illnesses if we are determined to work correctly with our mental processes and physical habitsKeep in mind that humanity has been exposed to coercive persuasion, designed to maintain control.

Be mindful as much as you can, embrace your inner potential, and analyze any beliefs about yourself being these the ones that create your future. If you are not conscious, you are probably creating the life that you don't want. On our planet, there are too many people living with good intentions but naively and unconsciously; even the ones that consider themselves awake have a long way to go. I started to practice mindfulness around fifteen years ago and I know that it is an ongoing process where you must put effort and discipline. This is one of the most important things in your life: to live consciously and in the present moment. As you master mindfulness, you will know yourself better and have more control of your life and what you create. Become mindful is an ongoing process that requires effort and commitment.

The moment is now, and it does not matter your age, it is never too late to make decisions that elevate yourself as a human being; think about it: if you are 30 years old, how do you want to be in your 70s?If your life has been going down so far, it will keep going down due to your practices and beliefs that are constantly creating your reality. This applies to anyone, stop looking for instant gratification and avoid impulsive behaviors that create alternative outlets. Life goes fast, and when you realize you are already old and experiencing adverse consequences that affect your well-being, like lack of energy, body pain, walking problems, and all kinds of health issues. Any deficiency in your life is the result of the limiting belief about yourself that you keep holding just because that's what you have been taught. If your life is not getting better, it means that you are not doing the right or most appropriate things to achieve what you want. One of my biggest concerns is about people between the ages of 40 and up. They tend to start being less receptive and behave as if they have all the information of the world, even we all can behave like that unconsciously. I have close people around my age, and I can observe how they have become stubborn and unconscious, which results in pain and suffering. I have been observing this for decades. It is good to understand clearly that the stubborn behavior and being unconscious is just a program that we all can change and. Remember it is just a program that you don't need; it is a harmful program. As energetic human beings, it is necessary to be in constant expansion, and since everything starts in your mind, the first thing you need to expand is your mind. And you can expand through experiences and knowledge, then this is the moment when you start to improve your connection with the infinite field of possibilities.

Reflection and analysis are skills that you lose with obstinacy. When you are stubborn you are acting more from your limbic system, where emotions reside. If emotions dominate, reflection and analysis are out of order. Be aware that being stubborn comes from the need for control, egoic behaviors, insecurities, and low self-esteem. All of these are unconscious behaviors that affect your receptivity, avoiding the capacity for expansion. I want to emphasize mindfulness as the key element for spiritual progress and expansion. It is important to accept that you are conditioned to be distracted from essential practices that get you closer to enlightenment, making you prey to a spiritual regression. Your spiritual progress is related to your material progress and your health as well. Understanding and analyzing what kind of things you support is crucial if you want to keep moving up. Many of the things you support appeal to your emotions and are not necessarily beneficial for you. On one hand, you observe progress in certain areas on the planet, and on the other, you can observe how decadence is taking over humanity. It is serious to see how many people reach a certain age and start going down as if it were something natural, and there are many beliefs about aging that go against spiritual and physical progress, like resign to exercising, lack of purpose, apathy, not trying to work out challenges on your own or stop servicing others.

The principles of the Universe are based on balance; therefore, you must keep your life in equilibrium, making sure you have productive days where part of your spare time is used to do constructive things. The reality is that just working eight hours and wasting your spare time with useless distractions is not enough to create a fulfilling life. Set realistic goals, create a balanced schedule, learn to say no and, of course, practice mindfulness to be conscious of the things that you do on a daily basis. Always look for balance. When you lose your balance, you create scarcity, health issues and all kinds of problems. As you balance your life, you balance your energy, bringing to your life the things that you want. Maintain your curiosity, understand that there are always new ideas to do things differently, and research about any topic of your interest. All these things not only keep you in balance, but they also keep you in constant expansion. Keeping yourself ignorant is a decision, and it is not a responsible behavior. Ask yourself what can motivate you to start making decisions that eventually will bring satisfaction and well-being. Many people are not motivated because they stopped being themselves simply to please others and follow the system that creates people who, most of the time, live unsatisfied. Being submissive and obedient brings frustrations and goes against your spiritual progress instead of having courage and authenticity, which elevate your spirit and eventually bring a lot of satisfaction. Remember, any behaviors are a result of programs in your subconscious mind, but any habits can be changed if you prioritize them. Your simple daily habits are the ones that create and control your life, and these habits are the messages you are constantly sending to the Universe and steadily creating something; it is crucial to pay attention to any daily habits and have the ability to analyze if these habits are bringing you the results that you want. Master self-observation, and your life will start to improve.

Every human being deserves the best, but if you want to enjoy the best, you must be prepared for the experience. Willpower is the key; it is the way out. If you want to achieve a significant change, you need to feel the motivation for change and set a clear goal, practice mindfulness to monitor your behavior and develop strength of character. The first thing you need to do to build willpower is to believe in your inner potential and understand the neuroplasticity of your brain to change mental patterns. Develop a healthy routine without putting pressure on it, understanding that it is a slow process, be consistent with your routine, avoid instant gratification and celebrate your positive results. When you develop willpower, you can experience more satisfaction, good health, and better self-esteem. In other words, your frequencies are higher, which is the main goal.

The moment is here where we all can become light warriors, acknowledging our faults but also our qualities. Light warriors must be conscious of how they really are, being this the only way to make the right adjustments. Light warriors live with faith, hope and love, are completely focused and disciplined, and are always centered on themselves as well as on behalf of others. Have the courage to be yourself and believe in your inner power, which is enhanced when you live under control and love yourself and others. Accept the present moment without being judged mentally and take responsibility of your negative outcomes.

Our planet is in the process of awakening where each one of us is playing an important role. Being aware is priority. It is time to be aware of what has been going on in this planet, it is time to be aware of how we have been mentally affected and, most importantly, it is time to pay more attention to your mental processes that are steadily affecting your daily life. Be aware of how important is to reprogram your subconscious mind, your bank of information which is tirelessly organizing your life based on your deepest beliefs and mental patterns. Prioritize changes in all aspects of your life, to make way for the person you want to be. Reprogram yourself to be more analytic to detect what is logical and what is not, and it is crucial to stop living your life so naively supporting things that are against your true nature. Take more time to investigate and get out of ignorance, and it does not exempt you from your responsibility of knowing what is correct for your life. The Universe does not understand if you do things consciously or unconsciously. It just receives your vibration. Ergon emotional Intelligence is about understanding how your actions and emotions affect your frequencies, it is the ability to analyze any life situation in terms of energy. This is a concept we can all explore and develop.. The moment is favorable for your expansion and improving your connection with the divine. Figure out how you really are and what you really want; make decisions and changes to bring you joy and expansion. Always remember that knowing yourself, evolving and expanding are the main goals in your life journey. These are the practices that will keep you strong and healthy.

Analyze what direction your life is going in without judging yourself, but with logic and common sense. Develop the capacity to be aware of your behaviors and become the best person you can be. Make sure you are happy and help others to be happy, which is different from trying to make someone happy. Be aware of things that interfere with your overall progress, such as doubt and fear, guilt and worthiness, or inferiority feelings. Instead live your life embracing concepts such as be an energy being, a light being, understanding that your exterior world is the manifestation of your inner world. And always remember that love and fear are the two basic emotions where love should be the predominant emotion.

This is the moment where we need more people living with good feelings and sharing the message of awareness to the world. Humanity needs more conscious people to create the great shift in the planet. We are all involved in these historical moments where every human being is responsible for the extinction of a malevolent system. You will never know how powerful you are if you do not work hard with your inner being. Be diligent, determined and tenacious with your inner job and eventually you will see the results you have always dreamed of. Infuse excitement in your life, live with confidence that everything is in perfect order, change your worries for gratitude and watch how your surroundings begin to change positively. Live with reasoning without letting emotions interfere and control your decisions. . Stop believing without understanding and stop supporting movements that segregate humanity. Be careful with excessive narratives, especially when they lend themselves to so many interpretations. Investigate, investigate and investigate. Love and unity should be your main goal, live in harmony with the Universe and your life will always flow in your favor. You all deserve to live in plenitude, it is your divine birth right.

Be aware of your thoughts, feelings, emotions, intentions and perceptions, these not only affect your vibration, but they also determine your life. Be aware of the great deception to which you have been exposed and decide to be part of the great awakening of humanity, all the power resides within you. Believe and validate yourself, expand and explore the countless possibilities of the Universe, you are part of this magnificent place full of wonders and experiences. Keep your curiosity, this one mean expansion. Develop a mentality of possibilities, being stubborn goes against your personal expansion. A mind that opens to new ideas expands and this is the general purpose of our lives, expansion A mind that opens to new concepts never returns to its original size. And most important Be Aware. A present creating awareness is equivalent to a promising future

I can hear the argument of "nobody has the truth in their hands or there is not an absolute truth'. But my personal conclusion is, when we choose our truth and practices we are choosing our destiny.

www.ingramcontent.com/pod-product-compliance
Lightning Source LLC
Chambersburg PA
CBHW071446130726
47997CB00006B/2251